SIMPLIFY

Family Travel

A **Reader's Digest Simpler Life**™ Book

Designed, edited, and produced by Weldon Owen

THE READER'S DIGEST ASSOCIATION, INC.

Executive Editor, Trade Books Joseph Gonzalez
Senior Design Director, Trade Books Henrietta Stern
Project Editor Candace Conard
Project Art Director Jane Wilson

WELDON OWEN INC.

President John Owen
Publisher Roger S. Shaw
Series Editor Janet Goldenberg
Copy Editors Lisa R. Bornstein, Gail Nelson

Art Director Emma Forge
Senior Designer Elizabeth Marken
Production Designer Brynn Breuner
Design Assistant William Erik Evans
Icon Illustrator Matt Graif

Production Director Stephanie Sherman
Production Manager Jen Dalton

Project Photographers Chris Shorten, Brian Pierce
Photo Stylist JoAnn Masaoka Van Atta
Photo Editor Anne Stovell

A Reader's Digest/Weldon Owen Publication
Copyright © 1998 The Reader's Digest Association, Inc., and Weldon Owen Inc.

Library of Congress Cataloging in Publication Data
Loomis, Christine.
    Simplify family travel / Christine Loomis.
        p.   cm.
    Includes index.
    ISBN 0-7621-0065-6
    1. Travel.   2. Family recreation.   I. Title.
    G151.L667   1998
    910' .2'02—dc21   97-53242

Printed in China

A note on weights and measures: Metric equivalences given for
U.S. weights and measures are approximate. Actual equivalences may vary.

SIMPLIFY

Family Travel

CHRISTINE LOOMIS

Illustrations by TRAVIS FOSTER

Reader's Digest

The Reader's Digest Association, Inc.
Pleasantville, New York/Montreal

CONTENTS

Enjoying a family vacation requires a positive outlook and a willingness to go with the flow.

BEFORE YOU GO...CRAZY

* —— * —— *

Simplify family travel? It may seem unlikely. But the fact is that any family can plan a vacation that is easy, stress-free, and lots of fun for everyone involved.

Simplify Family Travel dishes up a wealth of time-saving techniques, labor-saving tips, and cost-cutting strategies that I've uncovered in my years as a travel writer and the mother of three (well-traveled) children. In these pages I've provided checklists and other practical tools to help you choose a destination, organize your trip, and get support along the way so that your whole family can enjoy the best vacation ever.

Some of the most enjoyable vacations fall outside the usual selection of resorts, theme parks, and package tours, so I've included family trips that go beyond the obvious. For example, instead of staying at a hotel on your next vacation, why not stay at a working farm or visit a family camp that has basic lodging but first-class activities and fun? Whether you want to snorkel off Hawaii, hike mountains in Canada, or dig for dinosaur bones in Colorado, you'll find that *Simplify Family Travel* is full of tempting ideas that will send you and your children on more than one adventure of a lifetime.

As you plan, always remember that it's everyone's vacation. Giving children—no matter how young—a say in where you go and what activities you'll engage in will open the door to delightful new experiences. Best of all, letting everyone have a say instills in your family a sense of teamwork that will endure long after your vacation ends.

Planning a fun-filled trip is important, but as parents you must also consider your family's health and safety. *Simplify Family Travel* prepares you for the mishaps that inevitably occur on vacations and helps you prevent them from turning into catastrophes. You'll find advice on how to ensure your family's health and safety in unfamiliar surroundings, and how to cope with any emergencies that may arise.

If there's any single key to a successful family trip, it's a realistic attitude. If you're not always the best-organized family at home—whose family is?—it's unlikely you'll become one on vacation. The point of traveling together is not to follow an itinerary to the letter, but to share experiences and to celebrate who you are as a family. Refer to the ideas in this book for vacation plans that suit your family's needs and forget the rest. That, after all, is what simplifying is really about.

Christine Loomis

From the start, consider your family trip a celebration—
a time to revel in the company of the people who matter most.

SIMPLE SYMBOLS

———————— ✶ ————————

SCATTERED THROUGHOUT *Simplify Family Travel* you'll find a series of tip boxes that contain tried-and-true advice designed to make your next family vacation easy and trouble-free. The major causes of stress while planning—and taking—a vacation are worry about the workload involved, concerns over cost, and fears about safety. Ease your mind on these issues by following these timeless tips:

 Labor Savers help you ease the workload of trip-planning whenever it seems there's just too much to be done. Watch for these boxes to find out how to delegate jobs, share responsibilities, or to skip the nonessential tasks altogether.

 Time Savers explain how to shave minutes or even hours from planning and packing without compromising on quality, safety, or enjoyment. Vacation time is precious, so try to make the most of any time spent relaxing with your family.

 Bright Ideas, as the name suggests, are the kinds of insider secrets that travel experts rely on every day to make traveling easier and to nip problems in the bud. These ideas may sound simple, but important concepts frequently do.

 Simply Safer tips are practical, easy-to-follow ideas for keeping family members healthy and safe, whether you're staying at a five-star resort or having the adventure of a lifetime. There is no compromising on safety, but there are several simple strategies you can use to protect your loved ones.

 Stress Busters provide simple, surefire methods to make planning and taking a vacation easy and worry-free. These tips offer techniques to help you relax, enjoy your family, and take that well-deserved break from the rest of your busy life.

 Cost Cutters show you how to make the most of your hard-earned cash and create lifelong memories for little or no money at all. Wherever you decide to go, follow these tips to save money and enjoy a great family vacation at the same time.

 Rules of Thumb will help you prepare for a given situation by using tried-and-true formulas—including how much water it takes to keep your family from getting dehydrated on an airplane. These tips remove the guesswork so you're in control.

 Don't Forget reminders help you stay focused as you make vacation plans with your family. Advice in these boxes puts the essentials at your fingertips and helps you get it all done. Having fun is your first priority on vacation, so refer to these boxes to help keep everything you've planned running smoothly.

DE-STRESSING your
Vacation

———✳———

1 Take a **self-quiz** to identify the factors that are stressful for you and your family. **2** Review past vacations to see **what worked** well and what didn't. **3** **Visualize** each day of a potential vacation so you can find the pitfalls and eliminate problems before you start. **4** Plan this year for **next year's** vacation. **5** Get help with **planning**—either from a travel agent or other specialist, or from your family (kids included). **6** Create a realistic **vacation budget** so you know exactly how much you can comfortably spend. **7** Focus on family **stress points** (backseat arguments, tantrums when kids are hungry, tired, or bored) and design an itinerary that addresses these problems. **8** Give your **kids a say** in the family vacation so they'll have a personal investment in making it successful. **9** Choose a vacation that's appropriate for your kids' **age groups** so no one will feel left out. **10** Make sure your vacation meets the needs of **all involved,** including grandparents and family members who have disabilities. ●

THE LESS-STRESS FAMILY VACATION

CHOOSING A GETAWAY YOU'LL ALL ENJOY

* —— * —— *

Travel, by its nature, is an upheaval—an interruption of the familiar flow of people, places, and routines. Depending on your point of view, that can be exciting, stressful, or both. And while the goal of vacationing is at least in part to relax, the reality is that vacations—especially family vacations— often have a stressful edge to them.

The source of the stress depends on the vacationers in question. For some families, it's the planning that is most difficult. For others, it's getting to the destination. Still other families have such different interests or widely spaced ages that finding any common ground can be a test of patience.

Not to worry. You can have a successful family vacation —one that's low on stress and disappointment and high on enjoyment—no matter what kind of getaway you plan. All it takes is a bit of work and an honest evaluation of your family's strengths and weaknesses, dreams and realities.

TOWARD THE IDEAL VACATION

---- ✳ ----

THE FIRST STEP TOWARD DE-STRESSING YOUR VACATION IS TO CHOOSE A DESTINATION THAT FULFILLS YOUR FAMILY'S ASPIRATIONS—YET AVOIDS THOSE ELEMENTS THAT ARE LIKELY TO PROVE FRUSTRATING.

For some families this can be a tall order, but you don't have to come up with a solution overnight. During the next few weeks—while you're doing the laundry or taking out the garbage, when you have a moment at work, after the kids go to sleep, during commercials on TV—ask yourself these questions to narrow down the options: What's your ideal vacation, and what drives you and your family nuts when it comes to traveling?

Jot down your answers on paper or enter them into your computer. Looking at things in black and white helps make the issues clearer, and easier to resolve.

THINGS YOU ENJOY

What kind of vacation do you love? Some categories to examine:

Relaxing. This classification includes lying on the beach all day; sitting on the porch of a lakeside cabin reading that

The best vacations offer something for
every member of the family.

best-seller you've been carrying around for months; spa getaways; and condo stays complete with your own pool and/or hot tub and no compelling reason to sightsee because you've been there before or there's not much to see. In other words, uninterrupted peace and tranquillity.

Action. Most adventure trips fall into this category—ranch vacations, hiking, biking, rafting, and so on. So does sports-oriented travel: You can build a vacation around tennis or golf, or attend clinics and camps dedicated to skiing, snowboarding, horseback riding, windsurfing, or almost any other sport you can think of. You can even become a certified scuba diver at resorts around the world.

Learning. Want to immerse yourself in a new language? Learn to play a musical instrument? Take up painting? Find out how paleontologists dig for bones? Maybe

If you have more than one objective for your vacation, opportunities abound. Cruises, for example, can focus on learning, sightseeing, relaxing, and action.

your love is history, and you yearn to explore European castles, Civil War battle sites, or Egyptian tombs. Volunteering to assist with scientific research is a stimulating opportunity; so are nature studies or journeys into native cultures. When it comes to vacations, learning and having fun are not mutually exclusive.

Sightseeing. Is there one place you've always yearned to go? Do you love the

A Day in a Life

Avoid surprises by visualizing each day of your potential vacation. What will you all be doing? Is there adults-only time? Free time? Do you need a rental car? How much baggage is required (and who's carrying it)? Envisioning the realities, along with the possible pitfalls, will help you create a vacation that works for everyone.

idea of driving across the stunning heights of the Rockies? Riding a train through the hills and heaths of Scotland? Sailing around the Hawaiian Islands? Maybe there's a country that intrigues you, or a national park you haven't been to since you were a child. Or perhaps a commercial destination is your goal: Some theme parks, zoos, and aquariums practically define family travel for people throughout the world.

Reunions. Ours is a highly mobile age in which families frequently move. If you have relatives living far away or friends you've left behind, reconnecting with them may be just the kind of vacation that will help you get back in touch.

Variety. If you have more than one objective for your vacation, opportunities abound. Eco-tourism has become an increasingly popular vacation option, yet the experience can encompass everything from stays at spartan resorts or remote campsites to luxury tours that begin and end nearer to home. Cruises can focus on learning, sightseeing, relaxing, nature, action, or all of the above.

THINGS YOU DREAD

There are aspects of almost any vacation that can drive you crazy or make you nervous or uncomfortable. But if you identify these stress points far enough in advance, you can devise a plan to eliminate such trouble spots or have someone else take care of them for you. Here are a few of the stress points that may appear on your list:

Making arrangements. Not everyone enjoys making countless phone calls to airlines, car-rental agencies, and hotels, or has the time to do so. A knowledgeable travel agent can help. Once the agent knows your tastes, all you have to do is give him or her a basic idea of what you want and then just let the agent take it from there. It's one-stop shopping for lodging, airline or other travel tickets, rental cars, even meals and activities. A good tour operator or travel outfitter who books not only guided adventures but also airfare, lodging, and other activities can do the same for you. Or if you like some aspects of planning but not others, you and your agent can share the work. On the other hand, if you hesitate to turn over such a major responsibility to someone else, go ahead and do the planning— but get your family to help.

Driving with kids. Does the idea of being in a car for a week with your family sound like a nightmare? If so, try to pinpoint what it is that gets to you: The whining and squabbles in the backseat? Having to stop constantly for snacks and bathroom breaks? Your teen's choice of music on the car stereo? One answer, of course, is to avoid driving vacations altogether. That's not the only answer, though. You can plan a trip that takes your children's needs into account—for example, driving only a few hours each day and stopping often, or buying your teen a tape player and headphones. What you do depends on whether you just want to get where you're going or whether getting there is part of the vacation.

Stressful destinations. If cities make you nervous—so nervous you can't relax while walking around or taking local transportation—an urban holiday probably isn't for you. Ditto vacations in wilderness environments and national parks where bears and other wild animals roam. These inhabitants of the natural world won't be moving out soon, so if the idea of sharing their home is nerve-racking, consider an alternative—no matter how strongly you

Mad Money

To save money—and avoid fights every time you pass a souvenir shop—plan to give each child a fixed amount to spend however he or she wishes (don't protest that their choices are silly; that's how they learn). Hand it all over before you leave, or dole it out in a couple of installments during the trip.

feel that your kids should be exposed to the wonders of nature. The same holds true for vacations dedicated to sports or social activities: If you're going along just to make your family happy, you probably won't enjoy yourself.

Money concerns. The expense of a vacation can be a source of stress for many

If your kids turn into gremlins on long car trips, try stopping early each day.

Less-Stress Vacations

————— ✳ —————

THE BEST VACATIONS LET YOU RELAX, DE-STRESS, and reconnect with your family. Which is not to say that there's one ideal vacation. De-stressing for you might mean having the kids help you cook simple meals around a campfire. It could mean opting for a resort with a kids' day camp and a ton of activities. Whatever works for you is best. Here are some less-stress options.

	Good for young kids	Good for older kids	Cost-effective	Quick to arrange
Day trips from home. Often we miss what's great in our own backyards. Hike the trails of a state park, check out what's new at a local museum, spend a day in the city seeing the sights.	●	●	●	●
City escapes. City hotels, aimed mostly at business travelers, often have great weekend deals. Take the kids ice-skating, shopping, or to the zoo, a museum, or a fun restaurant. Kids in strollers and teens love cities.	●	●	◐	◐
Rustic getaways. Simple, affordable cottages or cabins can be found in spectacular places: at state and national parks, beside mountain lakes, on windy bluffs by the sea. With no phones or TVs, it's hard not to spend quality time together.	●	●	●	
Recreational vehicle vacations. Forget stereotypes: RVs *are* for families. Rent or buy (inexpensive to luxury), pack a few things, and take off. No itinerary, no reservations—just the freedom to go when and where you want.	●	●	◐	●
Family camps. Whether your focus is arts and crafts, sports, or nature, there's a camp for you—most with activities and meals set up so all you have to do is enjoy the experience.	◐	●	●	
All-inclusive resorts or guest ranches. There are no surprises, no hidden costs, no bills run up for daily activities and the endless snacks that are part of any family vacation. You pay up front and don't have to think about it again.	●	●	◐	◐
Guided rafting trips. River guides do it all, from hauling gear and cooking to ensuring safety. Some trips even include table linens and glassware. Your job: to relax—or enjoy a rush of adrenaline—as you follow the river.	●	●	◐	

people—and not just those on a tight budget. When planning a trip for your family, you have to decide how much you can afford to spend and how much you're willing to splurge. Maybe there are other things in life that you'd willingly give up for the vacation you really want. If not, and your budget precludes your dream vacation anytime in the near future, perhaps you can take a short vacation this year and go for that long, deluxe trip after you've had more time to save up for it. Or maybe an expensive trip isn't the answer at all. From a child's point of view, a weeklong stay at a family camp near home may be much more fun than an extended tour of a foreign country.

The bottom line is that you'll want to feel comfortable with whatever trade-offs you have to make between the money you spend and the enjoyment you receive. That may mean adjusting the definition of your dream vacation, but it shouldn't mean giving it up completely.

Kid crazies. You know your family better than anyone, so you're probably aware of all the things that can trigger discomfort and discontentment. If you know, for example, that your children need snacks throughout the day or else they experience serious insanity, it's a sure bet that this pattern will continue while they're on the road. If they're transformed from Dr. Jekyll into Mr. Hyde when they stay up past eight at night, that's not going to change just because they're having the time of their lives.

While problems like these can make traveling stressful, they're certainly not insurmountable. If you make an effort to anticipate these rough spots for your family, you'll be better able to cope with the stress points or plan around them.

A relaxing vacation *is a realistic objective for families with kids. The key is to consider in advance what each family member finds stressful or rewarding, and to set your vacation schedule accordingly.*

WHOSE VACATION
IS IT ANYWAY?

———— ✳ ————

ONCE YOU'VE DECIDED WHAT YOU WANT IN A GETAWAY AND WHAT YOU DON'T, STEP BACK AND REFLECT THAT WHEN IT COMES TO FAMILY TRAVEL, IT ISN'T JUST YOUR VACATION—THERE ARE OTHER PEOPLE TO CONSIDER.

Although ideally you should plan a vacation that appeals to every member of the family, that ideal is very tough to achieve. To one degree or another you'll probably find that you need to compromise.

Some experts advise parents to choose vacations without input from kids. This is reasonable. Parents have the knowledge, experience, and financial understanding that children lack. And besides, goes the thinking, kids can have fun anywhere, so why shouldn't parents go ahead and travel where they really want to?

Other experts counsel parents to build vacations around what the children want to do. The reasoning here is that if you manage to make your children happy,

two. Whichever of these paths you decide to follow, your kids' ages will be certain to have an impact on the choices you make. The following are some tried-and-true pointers for successful vacations with children of all ages.

TRAVEL WITH INFANTS

Babies are surprisingly adaptable travel companions. They're (mostly) happy to go wherever you go, and they love looking around at interesting sights. The things that catch a baby's fancy—people, animals, bright lights, other babies—aren't what make it to the list of top attractions in most guidebooks, but no matter. That means you don't have to do a lot to keep

Some experts advise parents to choose vacations without input from kids. Others say to build vacations around what children want to do.

there will be less complaining, bickering, and other behavior that annoys parents. There's plenty of evidence to suggest that this, too, is a reasonable approach, producing the desired result of less stress for parents and kids alike.

In fact, you can have success using either strategy—or a combination of the

babies occupied. Comfortable in strollers or backpack carriers, they can easily travel along city streets or park trails, and they can fall asleep just about anywhere, allowing you to continue sightseeing when they're too tired to keep their eyes open.

The biggest drawback to traveling with infants is the mind-boggling array of gear and accessories they require and the frequency with which they must sleep and eat. While it's a logistical challenge to make plans that fit around your infant's routines, it's a fact that sticking to regular eating and sleeping patterns will dramatically increase your chances of keeping your baby happy and contented.

However, it's also a fact that as soon as you get used to one routine, your baby will attempt to foil your plans by developing a new one. So be sure to create an itinerary that's flexible and made up of several short components each day.

Being able to make quick adjustments is key. You might all go to a museum in the morning, but if your baby starts to balk, be prepared to go back to the hotel. If he or she is doing well, stay in town for lunch. You might then plan to sit by the pool for most of the afternoon or arrange for the adults to split up for a couple of hours—one staying with the baby and the other enjoying a solo activity or special time with an older child. If you use this

approach, you'll likely have fewer problems than if you choose an itinerary that locks you into a full day's activities, hours away from your accommodations.

Flexibility is good for parents, too. Babies are labor-intensive, so if you can make things easier on yourself, go ahead. It's OK to give your baby an occasional bottle, for example, even if you're a fervent believer in breast-feeding. Doing so allows you to go out one night and leave the baby with a sitter. Introduce the bottle before your trip, though; a vacation is no time to surprise your baby.

Families who are flying should know that there are two approaches to scheduling flights with infants. If your baby is a good sleeper, fly during nap time. Your baby will sleep through most of the flight, won't notice changes in ear pressure, and will be well rested and cheerful when you arrive at your destination. If, however, your baby is unlikely to sleep in the midst of so much noise and action—and will end up overtired and cranky—book flights for the

**Kids and adults may have different definitions of fun.
Resolve clashes by finding compromises.**

longest stretch between naps, trying to leave the house immediately after a nap. That way, your baby will be in a good mood on the plane.

Contrary to popular belief, beach vacations are not the best choice for families with infants: Strong sun and babies don't mix—and if having to keep a baby indoors forces parents to spend a good part of the day away from the sun, sand, and water, they can feel shortchanged. As for those other popular destinations— theme parks—you should probably postpone this kind of trip if you've got an infant in tow unless you also have older children who are far more likely to enjoy the rides and exhibitions these parks offer.

Young children *can accompany you on almost any adventure if you keep a careful watch over them. Just be sure to take turns so that neither parent feels overburdened.*

So what does work? City vacations are ideal. You can visit museums, art galleries, zoos, cafés, even shopping malls when you have an infant safely secured in a stroller or backpack carrier. You can also take boat tours or check out marketplaces. Other suitable vacation choices are:

◆ RESORTS, HOTELS, AND RANCHES WITH INFANT-CARE PROGRAMS

◆ CAR CAMPING, OR TRAVEL IN A RECREATIONAL VEHICLE

◆ VISITS TO RELATIVES

◆ HOUSEBOAT RENTALS

KIDS FOUR AND UNDER

Taking a family vacation with two- to four-year-olds is one of those classic good news/bad news situations.

The bad news is that this is probably the most difficult age group to travel with. Young kids are notoriously difficult to keep restrained during travel, prone to embarrassing temper tantrums, capable of getting lost in a flash, and exhausting to both themselves and their parents.

The good news is that children in this age group are charming, enthusiastic, and insatiably curious—they delight in the smallest things. Those are the attributes of an excellent traveler, and vacationing with preschoolers and toddlers is more often than not a wonderful gift to adults. It takes a little bit of work, though, so your first job as tour leader is to slow down. If you take the time to view the world through your child's eyes instead of trying to get your child to view it through yours and go at your pace, both you and your toddler will be happier.

Young children often have difficulty keeping still and focusing for extended periods, which means that long travel days and an itinerary packed with too many activities requiring quiet, attentive behavior (eating out, some museum visits, and shopping, for example) don't work. Yet toddlers and preschoolers do very well when scheduled activities are short in duration and allow for movement and questions. Activities that take advantage of a young child's natural sense of curiosity and wonder—hands-on museums, nature walks, zoos, and farms—are ideal.

If you're traveling by car, try to keep the driving time each day to a minimum and stop frequently to let the kids run around. One way to make travel days fun is to arrive at your hotel or campsite early enough each day so that there's still time for the family to do something together—splash in the pool, take a long walk, play a game—before the requirements of dinner and bedtime crop up.

When traveling by car, try to keep daily driving time to a minimum and stop frequently to let the kids run around.

When you schedule flights, take your kids' daily patterns into account. As you do with infants, try to fly during nap times so kids will sleep through any annoyances. Or if your child is a light sleeper, start your journey when he or she will have freshly awakened and is less likely to be feeling tired and irritable.

Done Deal

Once you've decided on your vacation for this year, don't second-guess yourself. You've thought it through, done the research, gotten the expert help—now enjoy. This is not your last vacation, and you'll have plenty of time in the future to try something else.

Safety is a big issue with kids in this age group. They're fast, they're small, and they're oblivious to their limitations, which means some environments pose major threats to their well-being. Crowds, water, traffic, and wilderness areas are just a few. If your ideal vacation involves travel to such problematic areas, you should weigh the issues. Is the destination so perfect in other ways that it's worth being on the alert throughout the vacation? Do you have enough adults in your group (your partner, relatives, friends) to split watch times? Can you minimize dangers by taking preventive measures? A stroller, for example, keeps a toddler safe at a crowded theme park; a Coast Guard–approved flotation device is literally a lifesaver for children around water.

Another solution is to take only older kids on certain vacations. Younger children who stay at home can be rewarded with a visit to grandparents or a vacation of their own later. Sometimes, altering your plans just a little makes life easier.

If you're set on an outdoor trip but the hazards and logistics of a backcountry adventure are too great, scale down the vacation to a stay at an established campground in a national forest or state park. That way you can still enjoy nature but have access to roads, phones, and nearby medical facilities. The great thing about children is that they're always growing, and you can try different kinds of family vacations in the coming years.

SCHOOL-AGE KIDS

This is the easy age. Children 5 to 12 have the enthusiasm and curiosity of their younger years but are more independent and less labor-intensive for parents. They can appreciate cultural explorations and have the understanding and patience for more in-depth museum exhibits and learning vacations. This gives parents more choices as they plan family vacations. However, school-age children have definite likes and dislikes; they want to

Touring by bike can be exhilarating for older kids. You can take day trips from a home base or hop between inns or youth hostels. Be sure to allow time for frequent rest stops.

have a say in vacation planning—and they can be very helpful. They like action and entertainment. Parents will hear the dreaded "This is boooring" if there aren't enough activities and new friends to keep this age group occupied.

School-age children have a superabundance of energy but are often not capable of recognizing when they're running out of steam or when they're feeling hungry or cold. Meltdown can happen in a nanosecond, and because children themselves can't figure out causes or preventive measures (resting, eating, getting out of the pool or off the ski slopes before turning purple), it's a good idea for someone else to be keeping track of things.

Among the best vacations for this group are stays at hotels with kids' programs, a smorgasbord of activities, and lots of other kids; ranch adventures; llama treks (hiking with llamas that carry packs and gear so you don't have to); family camps; summer programs for families at universities; sports-oriented trips; rafting; cruises; or anything to do with nature. If you've been waiting for your kids to grow up a little before visiting that theme park, wait no longer. Now is the time.

TRIPS WITH TEENS

Caught in a tumultuous inner conflict between their childlike dependency and their burgeoning drive for adult independence, teenagers can present a challenge when it comes to vacation time. Teens often claim to loathe all family vacations (don't believe every word), and activities that they once found fun are now beneath them (or so they insist).

Peers have a powerful influence on teenagers' lives. In fact, the primary focus for any teen is hanging out with other teens. If you can't guarantee that your child will meet new companions at your destination, consider bringing one with you. Many parents have discovered that inviting one of their teen's friends along actually made the difference between success and failure on their family vacation.

Here's another thought: Vacations often provide a safe way to give teens the independence and freedom they crave. If the family is going to the relatively protected environment of a resort or a cruise ship, for example, your child can be free to come and go as he or she pleases, stay up late, sleep in, and test newfound skills without causing your hair to turn gray

overnight. By going along with this "hang loose" philosophy, you'll find you can minimize tension quite easily.

You can also limit opposition by letting someone else lay down the rules. It's standard operating procedure for teenagers to be annoyed by parental advice but to embrace that very same advice when it comes from (cool) counselors, instructors, and guides. Don't take it to heart. No one can replace you in your child's life, so relish the chance to let someone else issue instructions, and concentrate on enjoying your teenager's company.

The primary focus for any teen is hanging out with other teens. Many parents have found that inviting one of their teen's friends on vacation made all the difference.

What do teens like? When asked about their favorite vacations, they frequently list ski trips, cruises, and Club Med as top choices. Not surprisingly, these vacations have a high degree of activity, variety, and freedom, and the likelihood of encountering lots of peers. Depending on your child's interests, you might also consider cattle drives, rock climbing, white-water rafting, kayaking, parent-child wilderness survival courses, sports camps, theme parks with major roller coasters, city vacations, mountain bike treks, sailing, and snorkeling or diving adventures. Activities like these will get everyone's adrenaline flowing and can help parents and their older kids strengthen their relationship.

OTHER FAMILY NEEDS

———— ✳ ————

O F COURSE, FAMILIES ARE NOT JUST TRADITIONAL UNITS OF MOM, DAD, AND KIDS. THERE ARE MANY OTHER TYPES OF FAMILY GROUPS WHO TRAVEL TOGETHER—AND THERE ARE VACATION OPPORTUNITIES FOR ALL OF THEM.

These include single-parent families, multigenerational groups, extended families, and families with physical challenges.

ONE-PARENT FAMILIES

Among the hardest things for single parents to remember is that it's their vacation, too. They don't want to lose a single moment with their kids, especially if the children don't live with them full-time. But it's OK to spend some time together and some time apart. One way is to choose a resort where you'll meet other single parents. The Club Med family resorts are an especially good choice. Some even arrange a get-together where single parents can meet each other soon after arriving.

Another option is to go to a resort or on a cruise with a high-quality children's program. You don't have to use it every minute, but you can take advantage of it occasionally to get time to yourself. Guided adventure trips work, too. Many rafting outfitters, for example, run trips just for families, and the guides will give you a break from entertaining your children. This is also true of guest ranches with children's programs.

GRANDPARENTS, TOO

Vacations can be a way to create a close and loving bond between generations.

There are organizations devoted to this concept. The best known in the United States is GrandTravel, which offers several trips each year—all over the world—for grandparents and grandchildren.

Elderhostel and Hostelling International also offer trips aimed toward, or appropriate for, intergenerational travelers. Your travel agent can help you investigate

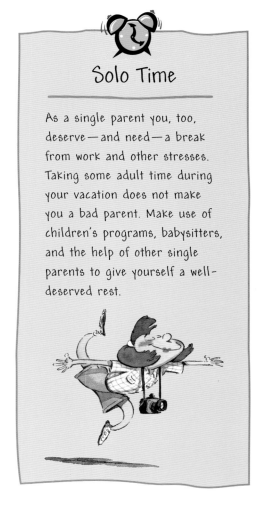

Solo Time

As a single parent you, too, deserve—and need—a break from work and other stresses. Taking some adult time during your vacation does not make you a bad parent. Make use of children's programs, babysitters, and the help of other single parents to give yourself a well-deserved rest.

these. Don't forget that groups like the Sierra Club, Appalachian Mountain Club, and National Wildlife Federation also have outings and camps geared for family members of all ages.

Visits to distant grandparents can be especially good vacation options for school-age children, who often develop a sudden interest in their family heritage. There are books and computer programs kids can use while visiting to interview relatives and record information about their family history.

EXTENDED FAMILIES

Want to get everyone together at one time? Have a family reunion. The librarian at your local library can help you find articles and books devoted to the subject. Many hotels and cruise ships are experienced with reunions and have staff members on hand to help with the logistics.

A family reunion takes a lot of planning, so don't do it alone. Figure out the main components—choosing a place, organizing activities, collecting money, fixing meals, and so on—and split up the work among those who will attend.

PHYSICAL CHALLENGES

Most members of the travel industry have updated their facilities in recent years to accommodate physically challenged guests, although some have complied to a much greater degree than others.

Even strenuous trips to remote locations and demanding activities such as kayaking are no longer out of bounds for people with disabilities. In the United

Intergenerational vacations *have become increasingly popular. Such trips can help kids strengthen ties with grandparents, whom they may not have an opportunity to see often.*

States, for example, Minnesota-based Wilderness Inquiry offers outdoor adventures for participants in wheelchairs and can provide sign language interpreters for those who are hearing impaired.

The important thing for families with special needs is to ask very specific questions about facilities and accessibility, as well as what kind of required help will be available. Families should try to offer as much information as they can, including details about the disability and the needs it entails, and the size and type of wheelchair or other adaptive equipment the traveler uses or needs.

Wherever you go and whomever you travel with, remember: Success is possible only if everyone feels accommodated.

ARRANGING your
Getaway

—✳—

1 **Delegate jobs** to your spouse and kids and let them help you plan. **2** If you use a **travel agent,** find one with expertise in the type of vacation you're after. **3** Before actually making a **commitment** to a vacation package, determine that the activities and facilities are right for all family members and that there are no hidden costs. **4** Let each child **choose** at least one activity for the whole family to participate in. **5** Keep your mind open to new **possibilities,** such as group tours or guided trips. **6** Call the hotels' and resorts' direct lines and **toll-free numbers** for information. If details differ, speak to the manager. **7** Don't give up on a **grand idea** before checking to see if it can work with some scaling down. **8** If you're taking kids **out of school** to travel, work with teachers in advance so your children can make up assignments. **9** Be aware that the **initial quote** from hotels and resorts may be high; ask whether there are better deals. **10** Buy travel **insurance** in case kids get sick and you have to cancel. ●

TROUBLE-FREE TRIP PLANNING

MAKING PLANNING A FAMILY AFFAIR

* —— * —— *

Of all the qualities you'll need in order to make your family vacation a success, the ability to plan is more important than any other—with the notable exception of a very well-developed sense of humor. With good planning, you'll be more likely to choose both the right kind of trip and the right destination, find the best deals and programs, solve problems and conflicts before they escalate, and adeptly handle any and all difficulties that arise.

Planning takes work, but that doesn't make it a chore. Brainstorming a getaway with your family can be fun—even illuminating—as you discover hidden interests and long-held travel ambitions you may never have suspected. Whether you work with a travel agent or plan some or all of the trip yourself, it's a fact that the more information you can gather, the fewer problems you'll have. And that's exactly what you want on your next family vacation.

WHERE SHOULD YOU GO?

———— ✳ ————

CITY OR MOUNTAINS? RESORT OR RAFTING? SKIING OR BEACH? WHEN IT COMES TO DECIDING WHERE TO GO AND WHAT TO DO ON YOUR VACATION, YOU CAN INVOLVE YOUR KIDS AS MUCH OR AS LITTLE AS YOU LIKE.

It boils down to three basic approaches: You tell them where you're all going and what you'll be doing, they tell you, or the family decides by popular vote.

Under the democratic option, family members pitch their ideas and make a decision by voting on the best of them. In this scenario, everyone in the family has pretty much equal voice. This works well if kids are likely to listen to the pros and cons of each idea and the concerns expressed by other family members. It's most useful for families with older children and teens who understand something about financial issues and travel. Very young children, who tend to have a difficult time objectively evaluating ideas and

who are likely to be stubborn about their own choices, would probably not adapt well to this approach.

A more moderate tack is to give the parents' votes added weight or to allow uncontested parental vetoes when a trip or destination is out of the question—say, because it's too expensive or inappropriate for your young children. Parents, in turn, have the responsibility to listen well and not give in to the urge to veto every idea except their own.

Some parents choose to do all of the initial research and then bring two or three options to the rest of the family to vote on. All must be trips the parents are willing and able to take once the family

In your race to get away, make sure that everyone has had a hand in selecting the destination.

makes a decision. This is a good approach for families with young children or whose children range in age.

FINDING OUT MORE

Once you've decided on the type of vacation, it's time to get to work finding the best place to pursue it. Helpful sources of information are chambers of commerce in the areas you're considering (almost every town or county has one), convention and visitor bureaus (a fixture in larger cities), state tourism departments, foreign tourism offices or consulates, and resort reservation services (most ski areas, for example, offer a toll-free number through which you can book everything from lodging to lift tickets to evening activities, and get other information as well).

Some segments of the travel industry have professional associations that can provide information about members in various parts of a country, although they generally won't recommend one member

Delegate, Delegate, Delegate

Parents who have a hard time delegating end up doing too much and feeling stressed. Get the family together and give everyone a mission—calling for brochures, reading guidebooks, researching airfares—and a timetable. Offer suggestions on how to proceed, but let the others do a lot of the work.

Check your local library for an encyclopedia of associations, which lists such groups; check the Internet as well for these and other resources. Your librarian can also help you find newspaper and magazine articles that have been written on a specific topic—say, traveling to Europe with kids. Unfortunately, periodical indexes don't

Use travel-industry associations to help you find guides or services in the part of the country you're hoping to visit.

over another. Use these associations to find guides or services in the specific region of the country you're hoping to visit, then call the appropriate members and make your own decision about whom to go with. There's a national dude-ranch association, a cross-country ski area association, and an association of river guides. There may be an association of people and places offering the kind of trip you'd like.

always include the most recent articles. Alternatively, try looking in magazines that cover the type of travel you're interested in; they're usually full of ideas and resources. A trip to the travel section of your local bookstore can also be helpful. Buy a guidebook or two that seem appropriate for the trip you are planning. Visit a travel agency or tourism office and let your kids pick out pertinent brochures.

THESE HIGH- AND LOW-TECH TOOLS CAN BE TIME-SAVERS—EVEN LIFE-SAVERS—FOR TRAVELING FAMILIES.

Travel software

Before you go, use trip-planning software to plot your route, find hotels, check out great places to sightsee—even locate ongoing construction problems. Once your itinerary is finalized, print it out and take it with you. Print one for the kids, too.

GPS devices

Global Positioning System (GPS) devices use U.S. Department of Defense technology and satellites to pinpoint your location. Units are self-contained or hook up to software on your laptop, and display detailed road maps. You'll never be lost again!

Cell phones

Phone-addicted executives may give these devices a bad name, but you'll be glad you have one when the car stalls in a snowstorm or when the kids are exhausted and you need to call down the road for reservations.

Maps

However high-tech you are, there's no substitute for a good, up-to-date road map, especially when you want to change your itinerary or need to find an alternate route. Spiral-bound map books can prove handy.

For computer users, another source is the Internet's World Wide Web. There's a lot of travel information on the Web, from sources such as tourism departments, ski areas, resorts, museums, and more. Many magazines, too, have Web sites or sites on America Online and other services. This is a great way to access a lot of information quickly, and most of it is helpful and up-to-date. But be aware that the Internet contains misinformation and some out-dated information, too. Once you find a destination or travel specialist you like, recheck or confirm the information, and ask questions to ascertain that what you've seen is really what you'll get.

You, your partner, and the kids can divvy up the job of gathering information. Older kids can write for brochures (they get to use their writing skills in a real-world situation, which will make their teachers happy). Younger kids can sort through the brochures once they arrive.

If you give kids real decision-making power, chances are they'll surprise you with how well they do.

Parents can make a first cut of guidebooks, then let kids who can read go through the material to get information about specific destinations. Allowing children to help in this process is an excellent way to teach them how to do research, a skill they'll need throughout school—and throughout life, for that matter.

When it comes to making the final decision, there will still be considerations that only parents can factor in: airfare or other travel costs, lodging costs at the vacation site, distance from home, time needed off from work, and the timing of school and national holidays.

Let children know from the start that these are issues that you'll have to resolve without them or that will be central to every family member's vote. Parents have to look at the tough issues, while kids get to make decisions based on what's the most fun. Fortunately, when it comes to family travel, these two differing perspectives can ultimately be compatible.

CHOICES, CHOICES

Now that you know what kind of vacation you'll be taking, you may face dozens of choices about what activities to try or what sights to see along the way.

This is a part of the planning stage when you can give kids real power to make decisions. If you supply them with a set of brochures and travel guides to look through, chances are they'll surprise you with how well they do and how seriously they take their mission. The bonus is that you'll probably find yourself doing things you would never have considered otherwise. And when the choice of activities is your kids', they'll likely be more enthusiastic at the destination—and thus better behaved during the trip.

If you're going to one destination— say, a resort, hotel, city, or national park —allow each member of the family to pick one activity that everyone can do together, if possible. It could be riding bikes one afternoon or going on a certain hike or

having dinner at one of those celebrity-oriented restaurants older kids love so much. It could be trying waterskiing for the first time or spending an afternoon at a unique local attraction. It might be the chance to stay in one evening, rent a movie, and order room service—with or without parents around.

Family members need to respect each other's choices—and no fair using bribery if you hate the chosen activity ("I'll do your chores tomorrow if you pick the train ride instead of the zoo"). When each child gets to be in charge for a few hours, the general attitude tends to improve. But if traveling groups become dictatorships, rebellion is probably inevitable.

If you're taking a driving vacation, sightseeing and many other activities will

If you let kids help *plan your route, you may discover fascinating places you would never have sought out on your own. And with a stake in the trip, kids will be more tolerant of any snags you hit along the way.*

be available each day, either during the drive or wherever you stay for the evening. You can take turns choosing these activities, with one family member in charge of the selection for a day or a leg of the trip. That way everyone in the group will be happy for at least part of the trip.

For example, on your older kids' days to choose, give in gracefully when they come up with a series of roadside attractions that have been the subjects of garish billboards along your route. Then, when

Years hence, you'll find yourself remembering—and laughing about— some of your travel experiences.

your turn comes up and you all head for a historic battlefield or the modern-art museum, your kids will be more willing to go along with the plan—if only out of a sense of fairness.

Don't forget: Even toddlers get a choice; read aloud the possibilities from

A relaxing side trip *can help break up a long day of car or train travel. Rent a rowboat or just laze by a lake for a few hours, then get back on the road. Let kids have a say in what activity you choose.*

your guidebook and be willing to live with your child's decision. So if you end up spending a whole vacation day petting llamas at a llama farm or chatting with costumed characters at some theme park, just go with the flow.

In years to come, you'll find yourself remembering—and laughing about— some of your family's special or funny travel experiences. That, after all, is really what family vacations are all about: creating the bonds and the memories that make each and every family unique.

By the way, parents are not infallible when it comes to choosing destinations and activities. If you happen to pick a dud, cheerfully admit it and help your children learn how to make the best of an unfortunate situation. Traveling always requires flexibility and a positive attitude.

USING TRAVEL PROFESSIONALS

———— ✳ ————

EVEN IF YOUR FAMILY THOROUGHLY ENJOYS THE PROCESS OF CHOOSING A DESTINATION, CALLING FOR BROCHURES AND RATES, AND MAKING ALL THE RESERVATIONS, YOU MAY STILL WANT THE HELP OF A TRAVEL PROFESSIONAL.

Why should you have someone else help plan your trip? A few good reasons:

◆ TO KEEP YOU FROM FEELING OVER-WHELMED BY THE DETAILS

◆ TO DRAW ON AN AGENT'S EXPERTISE ABOUT DESTINATIONS

◆ TO HAVE AN AGENT'S COMPUTER SYSTEM HELP YOU GET THE BEST PRICE

◆ TO HAVE ALL YOUR ITINERARIES HANDLED IN ONE PLACE

◆ IT'S OFTEN FREE, SO WHY NOT?

Unfortunately, not all travel agents and tour operators are created equal. Some are mediocre or downright awful. Some have expertise in one area but not another. An agent who worked well for your mother may not be best for you. These days agents and tour operators are like doctors: specialists are the name of the game. It's to your advantage to find one who specializes in your type of travel.

There are cruise specialists and adventure travel specialists, for example, who concentrate on that single corner of the market. Because they cover only a small area of the travel industry, they should be better informed about their area than a nonspecializing agent would be. Based on firsthand experience or direct conversation with families who have made the trip before, these experts should be able to tell you which ships and trips are appropriate for your family. They should be aware of children's programs and special activities (such as those on cruise ships or rafting trips, at ranches or resorts), or know whom to call to get the information.

Agents who really know the family market, however, are few and far between.

SIMPLY PUT...

TRAVEL PROFESSIONALS

consolidator • One who buys unsold airline seats and passes discounts on to travel agents and occasionally consumers. Consolidators may not be the cheapest source: you can often save as much money by buying advance packages.

tour operator • A specialist who puts packages and tours together. This person can book the land portion of the trip for you, or land plus air.

travel agent • A person who books airline reservations, cruises, tours, and trip packages for consumers.

Too often the average agent recommends the same old chain hotels for families because he or she has "heard that they're great for kids" or, worse, because the hotels offer agents incentives to send customers. Many chains do, in fact, have good family programs, but differences in quality exist from hotel to hotel even within a chain. General-service agents aren't always aware of program limitations. More than one family with a three-year-old has been sent to a resort whose excellent children's program starts at age five.

To find the right agent, start with family, friends, and coworkers. If you get the name of an agent who has worked successfully with someone you know—someone with kids in the same age range as yours— you're lucky. Under the best circumstances, a good agent for families is a parent who

has traveled with his or her own children (surprisingly, some agents don't travel very much). Once you've narrowed down your choices, ask probing questions to determine whether this agent meets your needs (see the checklist on page 130). You should vary your questions according to the particular type of travel you are considering— cruise, adventure, educational, resort, foreign, and so forth.

Make sure your queries are pertinent to your family and lifestyle. What ages are the programs for? How old must children be to ride a horse on the trail with their parents? Does the ship's supervised program run when the ship is in port or only when it's at sea? Write your questions down ahead of time so you aren't trying to think of your next question while the agent is answering the last one.

(see the checklist on page 130)

SIMPLE SOLUTIONS

DOING WHAT YOU DO BEST

WHEN IT COMES TO VACATION RESEARCH and bookings, you need to optimize your skills and place a value on your time. The goal is to use your talents efficiently and to your advantage. Here are several ways to accomplish this.

Simple Get into the challenge of researching your vacation and of making your own reservations. You'll know exactly what to expect because you'll have gathered the information yourself.

Simpler Take on only the research you're interested in and can do best. Why frazzle yourself searching for the lowest airfare, for example, when a travel agent's computer can find it faster?

Simplest Concentrate only on the planning that no professional can help you with—shopping, packing, dealing with the children's schools and your work—and leave the booking details to your agent.

THE BASICS AND BEYOND

⸻ ✳ ⸻

Family vacations today take in the entire spectrum of travel. While you have the option of returning to the cottage or resort your family has gone to for generations, there's a wide world out there.

Africa, Ecuador, Fiji, British Columbia's remote and rugged wilderness—all are places where families can find a warm welcome and many exceptional programs designed just for parents and kids.

On the other hand, families don't always vacation for the purpose of discovery. Sometimes the entire agenda is to be utterly relaxed and peaceful, and to forge memories together. A familiar place can promote relaxation and contentment in a way other kinds of vacations can't. Once your kids know the ropes somewhere, they depend less on you for guidance and entertainment, which frees you to relax all the more. And since there are fewer surprises

in a vacation spot you've visited before, you can sit back and start enjoying yourselves the moment you all arrive—and there's a great deal to be said for that.

GROUP TRAVEL

Parents who consider themselves competent travelers and are used to exploring on their own often dismiss the idea of tours, organized trips, and other types of group travel. Such regimented travel has gotten a bad rap in the past because of its "cattle drive" approach to tourism: herding folks through as many top-10 sites in as many countries in as few days as possible. And then there's the old rule that in any given

There are as many travel options as there are
families who travel. The sky's the limit.

Group tours *can get you into places that may be difficult or awkward to visit by yourselves. Here, visitors line up to tour Egypt's 3,000-year-old Abu Simbel temple.*

group of travelers there must be at least one obnoxious person who makes the trip almost unbearable for everyone else.

Though these stereotypes aren't without foundation, they are more likely to be the exception than the rule these days, especially in family groups. There are many tours and outfitters offering great trips for parents and kids. Honest.

BUT IS IT FOR US?

Still skeptical? Here are five reasons to consider group travel.

Time. Turning over leadership and logistics to someone else gives you time to enjoy your surroundings and your family.

Equipment. Experienced guides and outfitters have the necessary equipment, training, and knowledge to keep your family safe in the environment where

you'll be traveling. This may include a proficiency in the local language, two-way radio equipment, first-aid training and supplies, and other facilities for getting help in case of illness or injury.

Knowledge. Tour leaders and guides who have traveled extensively in an area are likely to know local people and places that regular tourists would miss or that would not be open or available to those traveling on their own.

Safety/Cost. Tours often allow families to travel to places or in ways they could not manage on their own, either because they lack the expertise to organize a particular trip safely (white-water rafting, for example); because it's difficult to obtain permits to travel to certain regions; or because booking such a trip as a private individual is simply too expensive.

Companionship. Trips that include other families give kids instant playmates, and they give parents travel companions

Introducing children to foreign cultures is one of the great joys of travel.

who understand that kids act like, well, kids. In a group situation there's backup and relief when it comes to dealing with children, including feeding, teaching, and entertaining them. Guides on family trips are usually experts in these areas (and in others as well), and parents naturally tend to help each other out. And, of course, when a tour is designed specifically for families, parents have less to worry about anyway because the itineraries, activities, entertainment, and meals have all been planned with children in mind.

Don't dismiss the idea of group travel out of hand, even if you once had a bad experience. Get a couple of good family-oriented guidebooks that provide a list of tour operators and outfitters who offer family-friendly trips (see page 142). You could find the trip of a lifetime among the listings—and have the experience of a lifetime to boot. If that obnoxious fellow traveler shows up, just ignore him.

FOREIGN TRAVEL

Families have the opportunity to take practically any kind of trip and in almost any part of the world. You may even be considering a vacation in a foreign country. Whether this is a good option depends on your particular situation, where you want to go, and what you want to do.

Introducing kids to foreign cultures is one of the great joys of travel. There are all kinds of people in the world with all kinds of viewpoints, experiences, and histories. Travel is a hands-on lesson in how different, and how alike, we all are. School-age and older children will probably get the most out of a multicultural experience. They can understand and appreciate cultural differences, remember what they learn, and become excited by history and by encounters with native inhabitants—human and otherwise. Children this age also enjoy trying a new language and often new foods. Structured programs in foreign destinations—for example, African safaris for families and cruises to destinations

like the wildlife-rich jungles of Costa Rica —are often geared primarily to the interests of school-age children.

Which is not to suggest that parents who have toddlers but want to travel to a foreign country should wait until their kids get older. If you're thinking of traveling abroad with a very young child, you have to look at the benefits and challenges before making a decision.

Destination is a primary consideration. While biking through Holland with a toddler in a bike seat is not so difficult, hiking with a toddler through the jungles of a country where tropical diseases are rampant and medical facilities are questionable is clearly problematic. You must also decide what you want to get out of a trip. Some parents may conclude that they really want to see the great cities of Europe and that they absolutely don't

Passport Priorities

Bring to the passport office or designated post office your child's birth certificate (original with raised seal), Social Security number (insurance number in Canada), and two passport-size photos. Children under 13 (16 in Canada) needn't go with you, but you must bring your own picture ID or passport; older children must apply for their own passports in person.

Before you lead your family on a foreign adventure, make sure you're all up to the challenge.

want to leave their infant at home. If your baby's easygoing, why not take him or her? Infants in a good backpack carrier can sightsee in foreign cities as easily as in domestic cities. Castles, museums, parks, and cafés are all the same to them.

Other parents, however, may find that it's just not worth the expense of airfare and the inconvenience of lugging along a supply of formula and diapers, considering that the baby will get little out of the trip. Better to stay nearer home this year and save foreign travel for a few years down the line, when the child is older.

RISKS AND REWARDS

Health risks are a definite concern on any vacation in a foreign country. Are conditions sanitary enough for a toddler who's wholly unaware of basic hygiene (as in, you shouldn't put your fingers in your mouth after petting a camel)? And what of illness and the need for medications?

After looking at all the possible scenarios, you may decide that the risk of illness—or the side effects of preventive measures—outweigh the benefits of taking your child along to a foreign country. On the other hand, there are international resorts in less-developed countries, places where health and safety standards are far above those of the surrounding area. You might decide to stay at such a resort and put off traveling to remote and rustic areas until another time. That way, your family can derive many of the benefits of foreign travel without some of the worries.

It's a matter of weighing pros and cons. Be prudent, but don't be afraid of a challenge if the vacation is something you really want. Despite any difficulties you foresee, it could be the trip of a lifetime.

Finally, give some thought to the cultural attitude toward children in countries you hope to visit. Some countries are absolutely kid-crazy, and chances are you'll have an even better time going there with your children than without them. Mexico, Egypt, and Italy fall into this category. On the other hand, there are a number of countries where, if your children act like children in public, you may well be met with sour looks. Germany and England can fall into this category. Such attitudes may or may not matter to you, but it's best to decide before you go.

TIMING

The two-week vacation that was once the norm in North America is becoming a relic of the past. Typically these days, vacations are much shorter as two working parents and their downsized employers struggle to coordinate time off. Even so, family vacations can be as brief as an overnight or as long as an entire summer.

The options for what time frame to travel in are equally expansive. Basically, if there's a time when all of you can go, there's a trip that all of you can go on.

countries, and many cities, for example— are perfect for families simply because of the destination, not because there's an organized program for parents and kids at a certain time of the year. No matter when you go, there'll be something for everyone to do.

What this means is that you can travel during vacation time and have the best selection of family-appropriate trips to choose from. Or you can travel at other times and find a better selection in terms of cost. By avoiding the crowds, you'll get a different, more intimate view of the destination—which can be worth a lot, even if there are fewer organized programs.

ROAD SCHOLARS

Depending on your priorities, then, you might decide to travel during the school year. Travel can be a superb learning experience, which is why some families don't hesitate to take kids out of school in order to travel. If you do this, be aware that

Typically these days, vacations are shorter as two working parents and their downsized employers struggle to coordinate time off.

Certainly, the majority of family programs and designated family trips take place in the summer months and during holidays, because that's when most families prefer to travel. There are adventure outfitters, hotels, and cruise ships whose programs run only during those times.

But there are year-round programs, too. And some vacations—great fishing lakes, living-history places, some foreign

schools may see things differently; you'll have to work with them so that your child isn't penalized for missing classes. The older your child, the less willing a school generally is to condone absences.

Talk to your child's teacher. Offer to pick up necessary homework ahead of time so your child can do it during the trip, but understand that most teachers are overworked and just as busy as you are; even

with plenty of advance notice, they may not be able to pull all of your child's homework together before you leave.

When you go to the school, have ideas for ways in which schoolwork can be augmented or made up for during the trip. You and your child should brainstorm together beforehand, because you don't want to suggest or promise something your child has no interest in doing.

When you ask permission to take kids out of school, suggest ways they can make up schoolwork.

One idea that real families and real schools have used is to have your child do a photo-essay on the area you're visiting. This is a combination of photographs and short sentences on poster board. It's more likely to be accepted if your destination is important because of its history, archeology, geology, culture, or natural history.

A trip to the city *gives kids a chance for real-life observation that no classroom can match. Have them keep a daily record of the things they see and do.*

Goofy's favorite spots in Disneyland probably won't qualify as a worthwhile project from the teacher's point of view.

You can also have your child create a map of your route. This can be a terrific lesson in more than geography if the work includes information about local terrain, distances between stops, travel times, vegetation, weather conditions, and so on.

Another educational activity for your child is to keep a trip journal. Depending on the child's ability to write, this effort can be a written diary, a combination of writing and pictures, or a series of drawings or photographs.

A very young child can put together a picture journal with your help. Have the child assemble collected photographs and drawings in a notebook, and you write down his or her accompanying story.

WAYS TO GO

---*---

WHILE THE CAR IS THE PRIMARY MODE OF TRANSPORTATION FOR FAMILIES, THERE ARE CHOICES TO BE MADE. HOW YOU TRAVEL WILL DEPEND ON YOUR BUDGET AND SCHEDULE AS WELL AS YOUR PERSONAL PREFERENCES.

There are advantages and disadvantages to every type of conveyance, so compare them and decide which allows for the easiest, most stress-free, and congenial travel (or as close to that as you can get).

BY CAR

The family car has many advantages. It's usually—but not always—the least expensive way to go. You can leave on the spur of the moment, there are lots of places to stay each night, and you travel pretty much on your own time.

Among the car's disadvantages, however, is that driving can be slow, boring, and tedious. You spend an inordinate amount of time searching for clean bathrooms in strange places. Motion sickness can be a problem. Depending on how far you're going, you can lose time away from your vacation destination. It's a fact: Kids whine more in a car than in any other type of transportation.

BY PLANE

The primary advantage to traveling by airplane is clear: It's the fastest way to go and the only way to get to some places. You can check your luggage and forget about it. Someone will serve you meals (if you fly at a time of day when meals are actually included). Kids love to fly.

Bathrooms are only as far away as the end of the plane. You don't have to drive, so you can relax and enjoy time with your kids. Flying makes it possible to choose a faraway place for even a short trip.

On the other hand, flying is expensive. Many aspects of flying are out of your control, including some that can threaten your trip. Weather delays, equipment failure, lost luggage, and canceled flights are a few of the potential problems.

BY TRAIN

The great thing about trains is that they make getting there half the fun. There's a romance to train travel that even young children pick up on. Kids can walk around

Waiting Games

If you have a choice of airports and are scheduled for lengthy layovers, choose airports that have play areas for families. Boston, Chicago, Denver, La Guardia in New York, Pittsburgh, and San Jose are among those with special areas in which to play while you wait for a flight.

in the aisles, and there's room for playing. If you book a berth, kids can stick to their regular sleeping routines.

Yet trains can be expensive, most notably in the United States. Some other minuses: You have to keep children from disturbing other passengers for extended periods. Baggage help is not available at all stations. Transportation from stations to your hotel or car rental can be tricky.

BY BOAT

Kids love boats of all kinds. Ferries can be a terrific way to break up a driving trip—and you can often bring your car, too. Chartering a houseboat or skippered sailboat lets you travel at an easy pace instead of speeding. Cruise ships can be a good deal if families book just one cabin, and cruises often have stellar family programs.

But as with the other options, there are disadvantages. Itineraries on commercial cruises are rigid. Traveling by boat can be expensive. Seasickness is awful. If you

Traveling by rail *can take you through scenic landscapes that are inaccessible by car. Kids can get up and stretch when they feel like it, and no one has to concentrate on driving.*

have young children, they require careful watching. Ships, with their constant excitement, can be difficult environments in which to maintain kids' routines.

BY RV

What's great about recreational vehicles is that you carry your lodging, bathroom, and kitchen with you—whether you're self-propelled in a motor home or camper van, or pulling a trailer or pop-up. Campgrounds are inexpensive. Pets can go, too.

The negatives: RVs may or may not compare favorably with other modes of travel in terms of cost. Most RVers cook and clean every day, which may not be your idea of a vacation. You may not feel especially comfortable driving such a large vehicle or towing a trailer that is considerably bigger than your car.

DOLLARS AND SENSE

———— ✳ ————

THERE'S NO FREE LUNCH AND, ALAS, NO FREE VACATION EITHER. IN FACT, A VACATION CAN COST YOU A BUNDLE. IT'S MONEY WELL SPENT—AND YET IT MAKES SENSE NOT TO SPLURGE IF YOU DON'T HAVE TO.

Most travelers know that some of the best bargains are to be had in the off-season, when poorer weather or the start of school makes vacationers scarce.

So when do you travel to get the best deals? That depends. Peak season varies from region to region. Summer airfares to popular mountain areas, parts of Canada, and Europe can be high. But summertime travel to warm-weather destinations— Florida, the Southwest, parts of Mexico, the Caribbean—can be a bargain. If heat isn't a big deal to you, why not take advantage of lower costs? Summer in the United States is winter in Australia and the Galápagos Islands (as well as a lot of other places), so travel deals are available. Yet you can see and do many of the same things as in the peak season.

weekdays (late at night, early in the morning). Weekend flights almost always cost more. Here's the catch: If you have to take off two days of work in order to get a midweek flight or book a midweek resort stay, and you lose either pay or vacation time, what have you really saved? You'll need to consider those factors as well.

SEASONAL SAVINGS

When it comes to lodging, consider the "shoulder" season—the time between peak and low travel periods. If you book a stay early in shoulder season, you can get a deal—and probably still have the benefits of the same weather and opportunities available during peak season. But sometimes programs are not available in shoulder season. At many guest ranches,

When it comes to lodging, consider "shoulder" season—the time between peak and low travel periods. If you book early, you can get a deal.

Midweek stays at resorts are often less costly than weekends; but city hotels that cater to business travelers have high rates during the week and bargains on weekends. The best airfares often require a Saturday night stay unless it's a local hop. You'll sometimes find better domestic fares in the middle of the week or during off-hours on

for example, families can cut costs in June and September, but there may not be a supervised children's program or as many children to make friends with. If you have older kids who would be out riding with you anyway, this is an excellent time to visit a guest ranch, as it's often less crowded and more relaxed than during July and

August. But if you were counting on a children's program so you could get in adults-only time, the money you save by traveling during the off-season may not make up for that loss.

YEAR-ROUND BARGAINS

Keep in mind that deals can be had at almost any time of year and that bargaining skills are not just for use in foreign marketplaces. At many hotels it's standard practice to quote callers the highest rate first. Reservationists are often told not to volunteer deals unless specifically asked about them. To get a better deal after a rate is quoted, ask if there's a better price available. There usually is. If you've seen a special deal in a newspaper or flyer, you should mention it. Ask about discounts for group members. You're likely to have the best luck bargaining with reservationists at the hotel itself as opposed to those at a nationwide number, but try both. If no one will offer a deal, find a different hotel. You can almost guarantee that your costs will come down if you negotiate.

After booking your stay, check periodically to see if new deals have come up in newspaper travel sections. Ask your travel agent to continue checking airfares in case of special promotions. But don't obsess about it. Vacation is all about letting go and being laid-back.

TRIP INSURANCE

Did you know in advance the last time your child got sick? Probably not. And it's a sure bet you won't know the next time either. In the everything-that-can-go-wrong-will-go-wrong scenario, picture

You can often save a lot on travel expenses
just by asking for a better deal.

your child breaking out with chicken pox the day before you're scheduled to leave. And then there's the possibility of lost or delayed luggage, theft of baggage or important documents, and medical emergencies en route. These days it's hard to tell which airlines have come out of bankruptcy and which are just filing. The same is true of tour operators. So what happens when the company you schedule with goes belly up? You're out of luck—unless you purchased travel insurance (some credit cards include travel coverage, too, so check yours). Most cruise lines, tour operators, and many outfitters will either offer a specific insurance package in their information kits or be able to suggest one. Travel agents can do the same thing for you. You will not get your best deal from those vending machines at the airport, so try to arrange for insurance when booking your trip.

Of course, some unforeseen problems are not covered by travel insurance, such as your boss's deciding at the last minute that this is a bad time for you to be away. Read the fine print so you know exactly what you're buying and what it covers.

Check with your travel agent, cruise line, tour operator, or outfitter for refund policies. Some offer no refunds. Others give refunds on a timeline—the closer to the trip date you cancel, the less money you'll get back. Find out what the refund policy is before you decide to sign up.

TIPPING

Paying gratuities is usually a voluntary gesture that's based on performance and service. Many people who work in the

Two Calls Are Better Than One

When checking rates, call both the local number and the nationwide toll-free number of the resorts and hotels you're considering in order to get the best deal; you're frequently offered different rates by different reservationists.

travel industry depend on tips as a major part of their compensation. Tour guides, for example, make a decent living only if they make decent tips. If you travel with a guide—in a city, on a river, on a walking or biking tour—you should tip unless the service is notably poor.

Some tips, however, are built into the pricing structure and are included on your bill. There are ranches with mandatory tips for wranglers and other staff, and there are restaurants that automatically add a gratuity to food bills. And with some types of travel—cruise ships, for example—tipping falls just short of mandatory. Exactly what's expected will usually be spelled out in the brochures.

It's a good idea to check guidebooks and consulates about attitudes toward tipping in foreign countries; what we mean as a thank-you might be taken as an insult in some cultures. And it's important to note, too, that some resorts here and abroad have a policy of no tipping. When in doubt, always ask.

READY, SET, Go!

—✳—

1 Make—and use—checklists so that you **don't forget** to do anything important. **2** Get the right **luggage.** Be sure it's suitable for each family member and the type of vacation you're taking.

3 Join **auto clubs** and frequent-flyer programs to take advantage of membership benefits. **4** Try not to go to **work** on the days before and after your trip. Use the days as buffers between work and travel. **5** Request **seat assignments** 30 days prior to flying. Check that your family is seated together. **6** Before you start packing, remove new purchases from their **original packaging** to save space. **7** Take along detergent for washing clothes by hand; if you can **wash** a few items while traveling, you can pack a lot less.

8 Finish your **"to pack"** list a week before departure time, and begin gathering all the items in one place. **9** Choose prints and dark-colored clothing; they don't **show dirt** or spills as readily as light and solid colors. **10** Keep your car's **backseat clear** of luggage. If kids have more room, they'll be happier. ●

PREPARING
AND PACKING

GETTING IT ALL TOGETHER FOR DEPARTURE DAY

───✳───

Preparing yourselves and your home for vacation needn't be a huge, overwhelming task. You can break it down into a series of small, very doable tasks. Prioritize your to-do list and then tackle the items one at a time—and before you know it, you're organized and out the door. Head off anxiety by following two simple steps: Plan ahead, and create realistic checklists to guide you (see pages 129–141).

As for packing, it's unfortunately true: Few of us have managed to master the art of packing light. Happily, wise travelers have been there before us and devised techniques that can make compact packing a breeze—not just for harried, hassled parents but also for kids.

One more thing: Don't be put off by the number of things in this chapter to do, buy, and consider. You'll find some suggestions more relevant than others. Customize what information applies to your vacation, and forget the rest.

COUNTDOWN TO V-DAY

———— ✳ ————

YOU'VE PURCHASED YOUR TICKETS AND MADE RESERVATIONS FOR YOUR NEXT
FAMILY VACATION. SO WHAT'S LEFT TO DO? A LOT. BUT DON'T LET THAT
GET YOU DOWN. THE MAJORITY OF TASKS TAKE LITTLE TIME OR THOUGHT.

And many can be done by someone other than you. Here's a step-by-step guide to accomplishing the essentials in the weeks, days, and hours before you leave.

EIGHT WEEKS AHEAD

Start your vacation checklists—What to Pack, What to Buy, What to Do Before Leaving, What to Do in the Final 24 Hours—in a notebook or on your computer. As you think of items and tasks, add them to the lists.

If you're going out of the country and don't have all of the documents you need—whether passports or original birth certificates—now is the time to get them. If it looks like the documents may not arrive until the last minute—or even late—show your airline tickets to personnel at the government agencies from which you're requesting documents. Ask them to put a rush on your application.

If you're traveling abroad, contact a travel health specialist (your health-care provider may have a travel department, or your doctor may be able to recommend a specialist), or contact your local health department to ask about immunizations and preventive medicines. (See page 143 for additional resources.)

With proper planning, you'll be ready to start your vacation right on time.

Arrange your car-rental reservations and reserve a child car seat, if necessary, through the rental company.

When it comes to what to take with you—be it luggage, sports equipment, camping gear, or clothing—now's the time to assess your needs. You can save shopping time and hassle by buying from catalogs; order now so purchases will arrive before your departure date. Here are some things to consider:

Do you have the right luggage? Think ahead to the places you'll be carrying your baggage so you can decide what you need. If you'll be negotiating lots of stairs, for instance, you'll probably want backpacks

Think ahead to the places you'll be carrying your baggage so you can decide what you need.

or shoulder bags. If you'll be flying in a small commuter plane at any point, you should be aware that many carry-on bags may not fit in the overhead compartment.

Families headed to the great outdoors should check appropriate equipment. If it's been a while since you put up your tent, do it now, checking for rips, broken poles, mangled zippers, or other damaged parts. Check the batteries in lanterns and fuel supplies for camping stoves. Have the kids try on life jackets to make sure they still fit properly. If you have child-size sleeping bags, test them, too; children have a habit of growing.

If you're planning a sports-oriented vacation, look at your family's equipment.

IT'S IMPORTANT TO USE THE MOST APPROPRIATE TYPE OF LUGGAGE FOR THE VACATION YOU'RE TAKING.

Kid-size suitcases

Bright colors, safety reflective tape, sturdy handles, and zippers that move easily are all desirable in kids' luggage. This four-wheel model flattens for easy storage.

Two-wheel bags

These are among the most popular with travelers, especially in carry-on size. Some even double as backpacks.

Duffels

If you're going on a road trip, hand out the duffels. They're easier to fit into car trunks and cargo space than hard-sided suitcases.

Canine carryalls

If four-footed friends are joining you on a camping trip, let them help by carrying their own food in a backpack just for dogs.

Take skis to be tuned, and have bindings set properly for each child. Check the condition of fishing gear. Clothing is important, too. Campers need good hiking boots, rain gear, damp-resistant warm layers such as fleece vests, and possibly gloves and hats. Going to warm weather in the middle of winter? Your children may have outgrown bathing suits and sandals since last year. Skiing? Be sure last year's ski clothing still fits. Note items in short supply—socks, underwear, shorts, pants—and stock up.

SIX WEEKS AHEAD

If you don't belong to an auto club and are about to use your car on a trip, join a club now so you can take advantage of member benefits. These usually include trip-planning services, maps, guidebooks, discounts at accommodations and attractions, and roadside emergency help.

Join an airline's frequent-flyer program, too—it's free. Make sure the names on your tickets and on membership forms

A long road trip requires advance planning. Examine your itinerary carefully to determine what food, clothing, camping gear, and sports equipment to take.

are identical, or you won't get mileage credit for your flights. Give frequent-flyer numbers to your travel agent.

FOUR WEEKS AHEAD

Airline seats are generally assigned and confirmed 30 days prior to departure, so call now to get your desired seat assignments and to make certain your family is seated together. Another call to make is to a kennel or other facility if you plan to board a pet during vacation.

Buy any home security and automation devices you'll need. These might include timers for lights and TVs, an alarm system, automatic plant-watering systems, and pet feeders. Figure out how they work now so you won't be scrambling to set them on the day of departure.

If anyone in your family wears glasses or contacts, order a spare pair today so they'll be ready by the time you go. At the very least, get an up-to-date prescription so you can take it to a quick-service optical store if glasses are lost or broken. If you need prescriptions or checkups, make those appointments now.

TWO WEEKS AHEAD

Some airlines take calls for children's meals as late as 24 hours before a flight, but don't wait. You'll have other things to do then. This is also a good time to buy childproofing accessories (see the checklist on page 133). Refill prescriptions and get an extra copy to take with you. Write down your doctors' and pharmacist's phone numbers in case you need information on the road.

If you'll be driving your own car, have a reliable mechanic check it from top to bottom (see the checklist on page 137). Plan the route now: Do it yourself with good maps and trip-planning software, or use your automobile club's trip-planning service. Clubs like the American and Canadian Automobile Associations (AAA and CAA) require two weeks' notice to provide this service to members.

You will want to carry a moderate amount of cash, as well as traveler's checks and credit or debit cards. Automated teller machines (ATMs) are handy because you don't have to take as much cash with you, but check with your bank to see if there will be ATMs where you're going. Buy the traveler's checks now, and be sure to keep the records detailing check numbers separate from the checks themselves.

If you'll need a babysitter during the vacation, call the hotel to arrange for one now. Ask whether the hotel can provide cribs and strollers; if they can't, ask where you can rent such items.

Check camera equipment. Buy fresh batteries and more film than you think you'll need. Resort-area stores charge premium prices for cameras and film.

ONE WEEK AHEAD

No need to pack yet, but get everything ready (see the checklists on pages 131 and 132). Gather toiletries, medicines, shoes, clothes, first-aid supplies, toys, and activities. Wash clothes and add to the pile. Make a separate pile for carry-on items.

Unless taxis or airport shuttle buses are available in your area, arrange a ride to the airport. You can call a car service or radio taxi, or ask a friend to take you.

> **If you'll be driving your own car, have a reliable mechanic check it from top to bottom.**

Arrange for your lawn to be cut, your mail to be held or picked up, and newspaper and milk delivery to be suspended. If you're expecting deliveries from a parcel service, make arrangements for those, too.

If any bills will come due while you're away, pay them in advance. You can also prepay some bills if you'll be gone a month or longer. Make arrangements with your utility, telephone, and cable companies, or any others that may tack on late fees or interest if you don't pay on time.

Call your child's school if it'll be in session while you're gone. Give the office your travel dates, and talk to teachers about making up assignments. Also talk about travel-related work your child can do to make up for missing school.

48 HOURS AHEAD

Plan to meet with a friend who will hold on to your house keys and a detailed itinerary with telephone numbers where you can be reached. Also, give the friend a list of the serial numbers for your traveler's checks, photocopies of airline tickets, and copies of any passports or birth certificates you're taking along. If you lose these, your friend can fax or send copies to you.

Finish laundry now. You don't want to be washing clothes at the last minute and worrying about whether everything will be dry enough to pack.

THE FINAL 24 HOURS

The day before you leave, stay home from work if possible—or at least try to come home early. Sacrificing one vacation day is worth it to reduce stress.

Once you're packed and organized, order dinner in instead of cooking, and use paper plates so that you won't have to wash up afterward. Before bed, load packed bags and any camping or sports gear into the car, leaving one bag indoors to hold last-minute items. If you live where it's not safe to leave belongings in a car, or if someone will be driving you to the airport, set everything by the door.

LAST-MINUTE DETAILS

Walk through the house and take care of everything that needs attention. In the

Eat, Sleep, and Be Merry

Keep young children on an even keel by having them stick to their normal eating and sleeping routines. If kids stay up late the night before you leave, they're bound to feel cranky during travel the next day.

kitchen, wash dishes, throw out the coffee filter, unplug appliances, and make sure the oven and stove-top burners are off. Adjust the refrigerator to an energy-saving setting, and toss out perishable foods. Take out the garbage. If you have canceled garbage pickup during your vacation, bring last-minute trash to a neighbor's house or with you to dump elsewhere.

In the living room and bedrooms, unplug TVs and other devices not on timers. If it's summer, turn the air conditioning off or to a comfortable setting for pets staying behind. If it's winter, turn the heat to the lowest temperature that will keep pets warm and prevent pipes from freezing (ask your local utility company for the ideal setting). Close the fireplace flue to save heat and keep out animals.

Turn off the water to the washing machine. Clean pets' cages and litter boxes; leave care instructions if they're staying behind and you've asked someone to look in on them. Activate control systems for security, lawn watering, and lights. Before leaving, secure windows and doors.

PACKING LIKE A PRO

———— ✳ ————

I T IS POSSIBLE TO TRAVEL LIGHT WITH KIDS—HONEST. LOOK BACK AT PAST
FAMILY VACATIONS: DID YOUR CHILDREN ACTUALLY WEAR ALL THE CLOTHES
YOU PACKED FOR THEM? IF YOUR KIDS ARE LIKE MOST, PROBABLY NOT.

Your kids will spill ketchup and spaghetti sauce on their clothes (especially on white outfits), and they will find dirt—even at the most classy of destinations. They will also want to wear the same outfit over and over, regardless of the outfit's cleanliness.

There are two ways to deal with these realities. First, do not leave home without a small plastic bottle of liquid detergent for washing clothes by hand. Buy a bottle just for travel, or fill your own. If there's one indispensable travel item, this is it.

Second, remember that this is a vacation, and it's not the end of the world if your kids run around in less-than-perfect outfits. Everyone else's kids will be doing the same—and you'll probably never see these people again, anyway! If you're visiting relatives, they'll love you and your kids no matter what you wear.

PACKING FOR KIDS

When it comes to luggage, everyone in your family (except babies) should be self-sufficient. That means having luggage that children, even young ones, can pull or carry themselves. It's easier to keep everyone's belongings organized when each person has his or her own bag. While many parents more closely resemble pack animals than people on vacation, there are ways you can change that in your family. First,

give children responsibility for part of their luggage. Even young children can pack their own carry-on or small backpack with favorite toys, activities, and snacks. You might want to set some rules ahead of time: only one stuffed animal, no snacks that drip or stain, no permanent markers, and so on. Impress upon children that they'll be responsible for carrying this bag. Let them walk around with it for a while; they may rethink their decisions about what to bring.

Remember that children get cold faster than adults and tend to be grumpy when uncomfortable. Pack clothing that can be layered for travel days and for changeable

Lighten Kids' Loads

Pull-luggage with four wheels on the ground is the easiest for kids to manage all by themselves. The reason? Two-wheel luggage requires the puller to leverage about half the weight; with four-wheel luggage all the weight rests on the ground, which means even preschoolers can pull their own suitcases.

PRINCIPLES OF PACKING

✳

PACKING LIGHT—WHILE TAKING EVERYTHING YOU NEED—is a game of trade-offs that can require a lot of hard choices. Is it better to take a raincoat with a zip-out lining, or a jacket and umbrella? Should you pack jeans and a skirt, or just a pair of dressy slacks? Tough as it is to decide, remember: No traveler ever complained that his or her luggage was too light. Here are some guidelines to help you pack wisely.

	Good for children	Good for adults	Postpones wash day	Lightens your load
Take clothing that doesn't show stains much. Patterns, prints, and dark colors can be worn longer and cleaned up more readily than solid- and light-colored clothing.	●	●	●	
Choose a color scheme and stick with it. If all your items coordinate, you can mix and match to get the maximum number of outfits with the minimum number of items. Plus, kids will be able to choose their own outfits—and always get it right.	●	●		●
Pack separates. They're more versatile, and they layer easily. If you get one part dirty, you can still use the other part. If you'll be dressing up often, pack skirts and blouses instead of dresses so you can achieve more looks with fewer clothes.	●	●	●	●
Rely on easy-travel fabrics. Cotton/polyester knits, natural/synthetic blends, hand-washable silks, fleece, and rayon are among the fabrics that travel best. Check your closets and dressers. What you want are fabrics that wash and dry faster and wrinkle less (or unwrinkle easily).	●	●		
Designate one outfit for dirty fun. If you keep one outfit for those times you or your kids are bound to get dirty, the rest of the clothing should stay cleaner.	●	●	●	
Double up on favorite outfits. If your child has an outfit he or she wants to wear over and over, try to get a second, identical one to travel with. When the first outfit gets dirty, bring out the second. Wash the first, and repeat.	●		●	
Remove new items from original packaging. They'll take up less space without their boxes and bags. If necessary, consolidate smaller items in strong, resealable plastic bags so they'll be easy to find when you need them.	●	●		●

weather and diverse activities at your destination. If you're going on a cold-weather vacation (including summer camping), take along at least one layer of moisture-wicking clothing as well as insulating and outer-layer items. And whether you'll be in the sun, out in the cold, camping, or at a resort, bring hats.

Whatever your destination, keep a camping-style rain jacket on hand. These useful garments are available at outdoor stores carrying children's clothing. They are lightweight and squishable, and often come with their own stuff sack. An alternative is a child's poncho. It's not quite as easy to pack but more so than a raincoat.

When it comes to actually putting all of your children's clothes in a suitcase, there are no hard-and-fast rules. Some parents swear by the plastic bag method of packing. If it appeals to you, try it. Just put a complete outfit—bottom, top, underwear, and socks—in a plastic bag so kids can grab a bag and dress themselves

Lost-Luggage Insurance

Pack carry-ons with at least one outfit per person appropriate to the destination you're heading for. That way if your luggage gets lost en route, you'll all be comfortable and able to enjoy the vacation from the moment you arrive.

without a thought or struggle. Even if you decide not to bag all the clothing, put at least one dressy outfit in a bag, with nice socks or tights, to keep it safe and clean for that special occasion.

You might also consider rolling your kids' clothes (see page 58). With this method they can easily pick out an item or two without having to turn the whole suitcase upside down.

It's amazing what can fit into a suitcase if you pack it right.

TRAVEL ORGANIZERS

✳

ONE OF THE GREAT THINGS ABOUT TRAVEL is that it gives you the opportunity, if just for a short time, to be utterly organized and free of clutter. There are many products on the market—some designed specifically for travel, others that you can use every day at home—to help you pack and sort all of your on-the-go items.

Zippered notebook *holds important travel documents and gives you a place to jot down notes while on the road.*

Net bags—*one per traveler—allow clothes to dry after wearing and double as laundry bags.*

Expandable zippered *accessory bag—with both handles and shoulder strap—lets kids carry their own small essentials and toys.*

Heavyweight zipper-lock bags *keep small items sorted and visible. Use one to hold a clean baby outfit in case of accidents. Use others to organize kids' underwear and toys.*

If you're traveling with a child who's still in diapers, take the diapers out of their packaging and use them to fill empty spaces in your luggage. They'll help keep clothes from shifting around. Remember to keep a full day's supply of diapers in accessible bags. To save room, take wipes out of containers and repack in plastic bags. A word about diaper bags: they come in many styles and sizes. For traveling, choose one with room for extras—extra clothing for the baby and younger children, snacks, and activities—in addition to changing necessities.

If you're flying from cold weather to warm, bring kids' jackets and leave them in the car at the airport rather than carrying them with you. Kids should be fine wearing a cool-weather item—say a sweatshirt—between car and plane, and it's a useful layer item for your destination.

can. Call ahead to see if there will be hair dryers in your hotel rooms. Even inexpensive hotels often provide soap, shampoo, conditioner, and body lotion. If you must bring your own, buy travel sizes or fill your own small plastic containers.

Take into account that you will buy things on vacation, so bring along an expandable bag for the return trip.

PREPARING SNACKS

Children have tiny tummies, and it's a fact that they get hungry far more often than adults do. Parents will save themselves a lot of aggravation by being prepared. That is, don't leave the house without snacks regardless of where you're going.

Choose foods that don't crumble easily and don't drip or stain: apples, grapes (cut in half for babies and toddlers to prevent choking), bagels, some dry cereals, cubed

Toiletries contribute the most weight to bags. If you must bring your own, buy travel sizes or fill small plastic containers.

PACKING FOR ADULTS

Because it's a sure bet that you'll be carrying more luggage than just your own, packing light is especially important. One way is to have outfits that double as both casual and dressy. If you take along one fancy necklace (moms) and one smart tie (dads), you can easily dress up casual clothing. Try to choose accessories that will work with several outfits.

Toiletries and personal-care accessories —hair dryers and such—contribute the most weight to bags. Eliminate what you

cheese, and finger sandwiches all work. As for drinks, be aware that flip-top plastic bottles often leak, so check them before you leave; thermos containers are bulky but reliable; bottles of water with screw-on caps are excellent. Juice boxes frequently shoot liquid out when they're squeezed; look for plastic shells that fit over them to prevent accidents.

Even if you order children's meals on your flight, bring substantial snacks. Your child will almost certainly get hungry before meals are served.

CREASEPROOF PACKING

✳

PACKING PROS SUGGEST SEVERAL WAYS to help eliminate creases and wrinkles in your clothing. The most important thing to remember is that wrinkles are almost always caused by the shifting of clothes during transit and by packing heavier items on top of lighter ones. Avoid these problems, and you're ahead of the game.

Try the bundle method *of packing: Fold outer garments around a core of noncreasing clothes such as underwear.*

Stuff tissue paper *into suit and jacket arms to prevent creasing. Stuff shoes with socks.*

When you pack suitcases, *put heavy items, such as shoes, at the bottom. Keep clothing protected by using shoe bags.*

Rolling *instead of folding can keep garments wrinkle-free and helps them fit more snugly in soft-sided bags such as duffels.*

LOADING THE CAR

---✳---

THERE'S THE HUMOROUS IMAGE OF A VACATIONING FAMILY PULLING OUT OF THE DRIVEWAY, CAR LOADED DOWN FROM TOP TO BOTTOM, STUFF SPILLING OUT OF WINDOWS AND STACKED UP CRAZILY ON THE ROOF.

The kids are jammed in among the suitcases, backpacks, sleeping bags, pillows, blankets, and too many pets; the perplexed driving parent studies a mind-boggling assortment of maps while the other parent smiles benevolently, if somewhat blankly, at the chaotic scene. Seat belts? Nope.

And then there's the image of a calm, well-prepared family sitting comfortably in their car with a minimum of luggage and a maximum of room. Kids have drinks in cup holders, and toys, games, and snacks within reach. Luggage is stowed in the rear, and there's a roof-rack luggage carrier to hold spillover baggage. The driver has a well-marked map; everyone is safely buckled up or in car safety seats.

Long to be family number two? Never fear, you can leave home as a calm, collected group if you agree on these points:

- ◆ EVERYONE IN THE CAR SHOULD BE COMFORTABLE AND SAFE.
- ◆ ALL LUGGAGE EXCEPT FOR DAY BAGS SHOULD BE STOWED SAFELY AWAY.
- ◆ EVERYONE WILL GET ENOUGH SPACE, ACTIVITIES, AND CHANGES OF SCENE.
- ◆ EVERYONE WILL BE PATIENT WHEN THINGS TAKE LONGER THAN EXPECTED.

LOADING PEOPLE

Comfort is not negotiable on a long family trip. If you want your kids to maintain a positive attitude, give them as much individual space as your vehicle will allow—it reduces backseat fighting and overall stress. Do this by keeping all backseat items to a minimum. Let each child have his or her own small backpack filled with fun stuff such as toys, games, coloring books, and crayons. Make room for a snack pack or small soft-sided cooler, placed out of the way but reachable.

Let kids know that they don't have to stay in the same seats for eternity. Plan on switching things around and giving everyone a chance to sit in different places. Just having a change of perspective can relieve the sometimes tedious nature of car travel.

Don't Leave Home Without It

The single most important item to pack for kids—especially on car trips—is a personal tape player, preferably one for each child. It can't provide more physical space, but it does provide psychological space, which goes a long way toward reducing whining and squabbles.

Assume your children will need to sleep in the car at some point during the journey, and keep travel pillows and small blankets near them so that they can nod off comfortably when they're tired.

LOADING LUGGAGE

Give yourself plenty of time for loading. You don't want to be in a position of throwing stuff in at the last minute and having chaos and discomfort as a result.

accident, luggage stored in this area could fly around the car, so keep hard suitcases in the trunk where they can be secured.

As you load bags, think about the order in which you'll use them. If there are bags you'll need every night at a campground or hotel, put these in the most accessible place—on top of other luggage, for instance. It's generally a good idea to put larger and hard-sided bags on the bottom so they don't crush smaller, soft bags.

If there are bags you'll need every night at a campground or hotel, put these in the most accessible place.

Put all of the bags you can in the trunk or rear compartment of your vehicle. If you must put luggage in with the kids, place it underneath the feet of your youngest child (whose feet probably don't touch the floor anyway).

You might want to place a soft-sided bag between kids instead, thus erecting a luggage "barrier" that might help keep the peace. The only problem with this is that it may occupy the space kids would otherwise use to stow their amusements and snacks. Keep in mind that in case of an

If you're using both the back or trunk of your car and the roof, give thought to what you want on the roof. Which bags will be easiest to get up and down? Probably not your largest, heaviest suitcases. On the other hand, if you won't be moving them often, putting the largest bags up there might make sense.

Consider the weather, too. If you'll be driving through rain or snow and you don't have a tarp or closed luggage rack, use the roof only to tie on hard-sided suitcases that won't leak (most hard-sided cases are

Everything you need *can* fit into the car—but don't go overboard!

relatively watertight). If you've packed the car and can't get it all in without burying the kids in the backseat, now's the time to rethink what you brought. Is it all absolutely necessary?

Keep only the items you can't live without. Doing extra washes, or living without something you might use only once, is worth it if it means keeping the passenger compartment clear.

And here's where your choice of luggage comes into play. You can gain some extra space in the luggage area by using soft-sided bags, which fit together more snugly than hard-sided ones.

If after readjusting and eliminating items you still have too much stuff, consider securing luggage on the roof (assuming you have a roof rack).

ON THE ROAD

Here's something else that shouldn't be negotiable: Use all available help when it comes to shuffling luggage. That means making it possible for children to carry their own bags (see page 53) and handing over bags to skycaps and bellhops. Having someone else deal with the bags frees you up to help the kids, allay fears, and check in without chaos. It's an automatic stress reducer that costs very little in tips. Considering the cost of vacations as a whole, this extra expenditure won't make or break your budget, but it can provide relief from strained necks, backs, arms, and shoulders.

You deserve the help. You lug things around every day. You're on vacation now —let someone else do the lugging.

THESE USEFUL ACCESSORIES CAN HELP KEEP YOUR FAMILY ORGANIZED AND COMFORTABLE ON THE ROAD.

Window tray
This sturdy plastic tray fits into your car's window and makes it easier for kids to eat and play on the go. When not in use, it's easy to fold and stow out of the way.

Neck pillow
An inflatable pillow with a notch for your neck can make it possible for you or the kids to sleep sitting upright with seat belts fastened. Buy one for each family member, or at least buy several to go around.

Activity sack
Kids can stash toys, games, crayons, and souvenirs in this multipocketed pouch that hangs behind the front seat. Even kids in car seats can easily grab what they need, and things stay out from underfoot.

STEPS to a
Smoother TRIP

—✳—

1 **Build your schedule** around kids' habits and routines, and don't plan too much for any one day. **2** **Leave more time** than you would expect to get to airports, train stations, or driving destinations. **3** Make car, plane, and train **trips fun.** Getting where you're going is part of your vacation. **4** When you travel with kids, expect to visit more bathrooms and **eat more food** than you ever thought possible. **5** If you're flying, **buy a seat** for your child—it's safer—even though the airlines allow children under age two to travel on your lap for free. **6** When using public transportation, **don't feel guilty** if your kids act like kids. But address any inappropriate behavior immediately. **7** On road trips, **keep kids engaged.** Let them help navigate, and allow them to change seats occasionally. **8** Dress everyone **in layers** for travel days. **9** Buy a **sleeping compartment** for overnight train travel. You and your kids will awake refreshed. **10** Maintain a sense of **humor** and let your watchwords be "Go with the flow." ●

GETTING
THERE...AND
BACK AGAIN

FINDING YOUR WAY TO
A HASSLE-FREE GOOD TIME

* ——— * ——— *

Organizing stress-free, comfortable, and enjoyable travel for the whole family is a matter of taking your family's basic needs into account—both as you travel and after you arrive. Each member of your family, you included, has a certain level at which discomfort or unhappiness occurs. Although those levels vary from person to person and from age to age, people's needs are pretty much the same.

Everyone must eat, sleep, and go to the bathroom. No one wants to feel too hot or too cold or to sit for hours in a single place. And while activity and excitement are what many vacations are all about, doing *too* much can be exhausting instead of rejuvenating. When nap time comes around, a comfortable, quiet place to curl up is an absolute necessity.

How do you accommodate all these needs and still have a terrific time? Relax—it's easier than you think.

Planning an Itinerary That Works

‒‒‒‒‒ ✳ ‒‒‒‒‒

I**F THERE IS ONE MISTAKE PARENTS MAKE ON VACATION, IT'S OVERSCHEDULING. THEY DON'T DO THIS TO RUN THE FAMILY RAGGED. THEY DO IT BECAUSE THERE'S SO LITTLE TIME AND SO MUCH TO FIT INTO IT.**

More important, perhaps, is to realize that when you overschedule vacation activities, you're merely re-creating the same frenetic atmosphere you went on vacation to get away from. Armed with that thought, you can start planning your vacation itinerary. It's a simple, step-by-step process.

Step 1. Gather your family and let every person make suggestions for vacation activities (see page 31). Write all of them down—even the most outlandish. You may not think that digging to China at the seashore is worthwhile, but your youngest might. Make each family member feel his or her ideas are important.

Step 2. Put a star by those activities that are musts; ideally, each family member gets to choose one activity for the group. If your son chooses the "dig to China" option, slate an afternoon to laze at the beach—and have him dig to his heart's content with pail and shovel.

Step 3. Prioritize any other activities. Consider the time, expense, and distance from your accommodations, any skills required, and whether or not the whole family can participate. It's OK to have some activities where the troops split up. But shared activities are important: Make sure you schedule plenty of time together.

**Having a good time is more important
than racing from activity to activity.**

Step 4. Eliminate activities until you have narrowed the list to no more than two per vacation day. Of course, the final schedule need not include even that many.

Step 5. On vacations of a week or less, add at least one morning and one afternoon of doing nothing; or, on a weeklong vacation, leave free one whole day, plus one morning or afternoon. Otherwise, you may return from your adventure more exhausted than when you started.

Step 6. Write up a provisional day-by-day itinerary (see the sample on pages 138–139). If you rely on your initial brainstorming list without fitting it to a schedule, someone will be disappointed when there isn't time to do everything.

Step 7. Review your provisional list. If you get a headache just thinking about all that running around, the schedule is too full. If you look at the schedule and think, "Gee, we're going to be bored," add back an item or two from those you eliminated. But remember: Sitting with absolutely nothing to do and nowhere to go is not boring—it's restful and revitalizing.

As you fine-tune your vacation schedule, also remember that it's the small, easy things that make kids happiest. If you're

Lazy Days

Build free time into your vacation schedule; don't just hope it will magically appear. Actually plan certain times when the family will do absolutely nothing but relax and enjoy each other and the surroundings.

Adults and kids tend to differ on this issue. But even so, your kids will still be happy —and you'll feel much more relaxed—if you skip the amusement park one day and hang out by the hotel pool instead. Besides, you'll save yourself a day's entry fees—no small sum.

GO WITH THE FLOW

While you're shaping your itinerary, try to take into consideration your kids' natural habits and routines. If you don't obey these laws of nature, you're setting yourself up for a vacation filled with frustration. You will spend money on activities that turn out dismally or you'll cut them short because the kids are cranky. Or you'll

Remember: Sitting with absolutely nothing to do and nowhere to go is not boring—it's restful and revitalizing.

vacationing near a theme park, for example, your itinerary doesn't need to include a visit to the park every day. After all, how many times can you get whirled around in a giant teacup and still find it amusing?

spend more time than you should pleading with your children to stop complaining. Of course, some whining and protesting are to be expected on vacation—just as they are at home—simply because kids

Don't let all *that fun make your family forget to take a break and refuel. Lunch doesn't require fancy menus or even a table. Just grab a seat—or a towel—and stop to eat.*

are kids. But the goal, a very achievable one, is to reduce less-than-desirable behavior to an absolute minimum.

There's nothing worse than subjecting yourself to an unpleasantness that could have been prevented with a little bit more planning. You're not only unhappy—you feel guilty on top of it.

Scrutinize your provisional itinerary hour by hour for compatibility with your kids' routines. First and foremost, make sure that your plan allows for free time at the right time, as in *before* your kids need to eat or rest. If it does, you've done your job well. But if you don't schedule the first opportunity to break for a bite to eat until an hour after the kids' normal lunchtime, disaster is a predictable result.

Anticipating the need for snacks can help. An all-day snorkeling trip or a four-hour sightseeing tour in the hot sun may

be a challenge, but by looking ahead, you'll know to bring snacks that will stay fresh and keep everyone going.

Schedule your days to provide ready access to restaurants, hotel rooms, or even tents at times when kids need to eat and rest. That means being near enough that you can get there quickly if your kids "lose it" even earlier than you expected.

Avoid scheduling outings that last too long for your family. If your youngest child can't handle a daylong trip, adjust

What children really want more than anything on vacation is time with you in a relaxed, happy atmosphere.

the plan. Leave your little one with a babysitter, or split up and have one parent stay with the child that day.

Activities that conflict with nap time or bedtime are risky. You can get away with one or two of these, but too many days of long, irregular hours are bound to cause trouble. And you often can't get young children to change their schedules to help you out. Is there room for switching, substituting, or postponing activities if kids have a bad day? The more flexibility you have, the better.

For activities you don't want to give up, minimize the negatives by providing extra rest (schedule these activities after a free day) or by making special arrangements (ask guides on all-day hikes to stop earlier than usual for lunch, for example).

TIME MANAGEMENT

Obviously, the need to retain regular eating and sleeping schedules is paramount with infants, toddlers, and preschoolers. But don't forget that even older children and teens need some routines, too. They do not regulate themselves very well,

especially if they're having a great time. Suddenly, without warning, they're starving or drop-dead tired, and you weren't planning to be back at the hotel for two hours because they swore they could handle it. Don't believe them. Keep the hotel shuttle schedule with you (just in case), or ask for the name of a local restaurant or nearby café where your teen can sit while you finish shopping or sightseeing.

Remember, too, that what children want more than anything on vacation is time with you in a relaxed, happy atmosphere. Sure, they love the excitement and thrill of meeting life-size cartoon characters and scaring themselves silly on roller coasters. But when it comes down to it, all they really want is love and attention from their parents. And you don't have to schedule a thing to give them that.

SIMPLE SOLUTIONS

THE LONG AND WINDING ROAD

YOU CAN BE FREEWHEELING, or you can be highly organized. There's no right or wrong way to travel; it's simply a matter of what method works best for you and your family. Determine your preference, then plan accordingly—or just hit the trail.

Simple

Map out your itinerary, decide on a set number of miles you'll drive each day, and make the necessary reservations. Spend your time on the road enjoying the scenery.

Simpler

Carry a campground directory or guidebook, and call for reservations when you get a feel for how long you want to drive and where you want to end up that afternoon.

Simplest

Stop each day whenever you feel like it, so you're not tied to particular reservations or a particular mileage. This is the way to discover great places that you might never have known about.

TRANSPORTATION MADE EASY

---- ✴ ----

A VACATION DOESN'T START WHEN YOU GET TO WHERE YOU'RE GOING; IT STARTS THE MOMENT YOU WALK OUT THE DOOR. HOWEVER YOU TRAVEL TO AND FROM YOUR DESTINATION, THAT'S PART OF YOUR VACATION, TOO.

Which immediately makes it an adventure rather than a hurdle you need to get over before you can start having fun.

Regardless of your chosen mode of transportation, there are a few things parents can do to make traveling time the best it can be. Always leave more time than you think you need to get to the airport or train station or to drive to your final destination. Expect to make more stops, visit more bathrooms, and eat far more frequently than you ever would if you were traveling without kids.

Keep your traveling time on any given day to a minimum. This isn't always possible when flying, but try at least to book flights that arrive relatively early. At the end of a travel day, leave free time for a swim or a walk if you wish, but avoid making plans to meet friends, go out to dinner, see a show, or do anything that you can't back out of once you arrive. A little downtime will prepare your family for the adventures to come.

IN THE AIR

Kids love airplanes and airports. Which is another good reason to get to the airport early. Children have a seemingly endless capacity to sit in front of a window and watch airplanes come and go. That's to say nothing of baggage going in and out, fuel trucks and catering trucks, de-icers—you name it, they're fascinated by it. Kids also have a seemingly endless capacity to move like molasses. They can take an excruciatingly long time to walk from the car to the terminal, the door of the terminal to

SIMPLY PUT...

FLIGHT FACTS

direct flight • The airplane goes directly from point A (where you get on) to point B (where you get off), but it makes at least one stop in between, which can add significantly to your travel time.

nonstop flight • The airplane goes from point A to point B without stopping anywhere in between, which makes for a longer individual flight but a shorter overall travel time.

meal flight • Breakfast and lunch vary the most on meal flights, ranging from substantial to nonexistent. By calling ahead, you can order special meals such as fruit plates.

the concourse, and the concourse to the gate. Moving like molasses isn't so bad, as long as you allow extra time. If there's no need to rush, you'll be in a better frame of mind when you board the plane.

There is a difference of opinion as to which airplane seats are best for families. Many experts suggest bulkhead seats because they have floor space where kids can stand, play, and fidget. The wall near these seats is also where bassinets attach, if you're using one. However, bulkheads have no underseat storage, and the armrests usually don't raise up, which means children can't stretch out across the seats and nap. And because the tray tables are folded inside the armrests, they present a finger-pinching hazard for kids.

The other popular seating option for families is to book a window and an aisle seat, in the hope that the middle seat will remain open. Sometimes this trick works, but sometimes it doesn't.

If your child is four years old or younger, bring a car safety seat on board with you. Unlike airplane seats, car safety seats have headrests so tired kids can lean and sleep comfortably during the flight. While most car seats are approved by the

Now Hear This

If your child has never flown before, there are things adults take for granted that can be scary to small children. These include the noise of landing gear going up and down, routine preflight safety talks, the noise of lavatory toilets flushing, and the sound of the brakes when landing. Let kids know ahead of time that all of this is routine and nothing to worry about.

Federal Aviation Administration for air travel, check to make sure that yours has a label indicating so. And measure your car seat; those wider than 17 to 18 inches (43–45cm) may not actually fit in some coach-class airplane seats.

As long as we're talking about safety, it's important to note that if it's at all possible, you should buy a ticket for your baby or toddler even if the airlines permit "lap children"—children under age two weighing less than 40 pounds (18kg)— at no charge. The truth is, unrestrained

Getting there is all part of the adventure.

Water, Water, Everywhere

Traveling, especially by plane, can be dehydrating. The rule of thumb is to drink one glass of water per hour of flight time. Carbonated drinks, caffeine, and alcohol do not do the trick.

babies and toddlers are at risk for injury or death not only in the event of a crash but also during periods of air turbulence, because parents can't always hold on to small children during these times.

If you absolutely cannot afford to buy a separate ticket for your child, ask for flights that are most likely to be under-booked so you can secure your baby in an unoccupied seat. Generally your best bets are flights that depart during the day mid-week or Saturday, or those that take off early in the morning or late at night.

When it comes to meals, some airlines have a bizarre sense of when their passen-gers need to eat; flights that coincide with what most people would consider meal-times are "snack flights" to them. And because it's increasingly hard to book nonstop flights, you often end up flying two short hops with no time for a meal on either flight or in between flights.

That said, do be sure to order chil-dren's meals if they are available; ideally, order them when you book your flight. Children's meals usually consist of foods with kid appeal—hot dogs or finger-size chicken pieces, for example. When you order special meals, you can usually get them at the start of the meal service rather than waiting until your row is served, which is good news for hungry kids.

If you're flying with a baby, you should plan on nursing or providing bottles dur-ing both takeoff and landing to decrease ear pressure. Do not, however, attempt to give bottle after bottle of milk or formula in an effort to stop your baby from cry-ing; it's a sure way to give an infant an upset stomach—and more reason to wail.

If you're planning to mix formula on the plane, bring bottled water with you. Airplane water is generally treated with

Be sure to order children's meals if available; they usually consist of foods with kid appeal.

chemicals and can upset a baby's sensitive digestive tract. One more word about babies: Airplanes are dehydrating, but because infants tend to get more liquids than the rest of us, extra liquids may not be necessary. Ask your pediatrician.

One of the downsides to flying can be the attitude of fellow passengers and flight attendants toward families with children. Some people consider you second-class citizens when it comes to flying. Part of the problem lies with parents, unfortunately. If you let your kids kick the seat in front of them, run up and down the aisles, and screech nonstop, you won't be popular with anyone on the plane and you'll give flying families a bad name.

On the other hand, it's unreasonable for adults to be annoyed by children who are just being children. If your baby cries as a result of ear pressure, for example, don't feel guilty. If your child hums, stares at people, or gets cranky from being confined, don't feel guilty. Children are not small adults, and it's unfair to expect them to act in a way that's beyond their years.

It's important to take action immediately, though, if your child is behaving badly. You'll score points with other passengers by telling your child—in a calm, quiet voice—that the behavior isn't acceptable. Also try walking the aisles a few times with an unhappy child.

Sometimes a brief change of scenery does the trick. Offering snacks and giving children your undivided attention are also good bets for stopping kids' unruly behavior and calming them down.

ON THE ROAD

Ask adults about the childhood vacation they remember most, and the answer is likely to be a road trip. The destinations of those trips might have varied, but nostalgia for cross-country travel with one's family is something many of us share. The

---

SIMPLE SOLUTIONS

STRESS-FREE DEPARTURES

You've spent hours making your vacation plans so that your trip will be relaxing. Why should the drive to the airport be a hassle? Plan properly, and you can not only make your departure less frantic but also save time, effort, money, or all three.

Simple

Drive your family to the airport, use long-term parking, and take a shuttle to the terminal. Leave time for the shuttle, and plan to load and unload kids and luggage more than once.

Simpler

Drive your family to the airport; drop the kids, your spouse, and luggage off curbside; then put the car in long-term parking. You'll save time and effort—and unload just once.

Simplest

Have a friend drive you in your car to the airport, drop you off (on the convenient departure level of the terminal), and pick you up; or take a car service, taxi, or shuttle both ways.

Traveling along back roads *can give kids a better feel for the landscape than sticking to the major highways and rest stops.*

road trip you take with your kids today may be the one they remember when they look back on their own favorite vacations.

When you travel by car, you get a feel for the country—its richness and diversity, its dramatic landscapes, its small towns and big cities, farms, ranches, and wilderness areas. If you take the time to share interesting regional information with your

road-trip blues, stop every 2 hours and let your kids run around for at least 10 minutes. If they can't expend energy in a positive way, they'll do it negatively—by whining or bickering.

Try not to be autocratic about bathroom breaks; you can't regulate your child's body. Do remind kids to use the bathroom when you're at gas stations or rest stops, but count on the fact that you'll have to stop at some unscheduled times.

For everyone's well-being, limit driving time to eight hours a day at the most. Six or even four hours is even better—not just for kids but for parents, too.

Prevent boredom by giving the kids a new perspective. Switch seats occasionally and let older kids take turns riding in the front (unless you have a passenger-side airbag; see page 92) while you join the gang in the backseat.

Finally, stop before dark so you can check in or set up camp and still have dinner at your kids' normal time.

How you organize your drive will depend on your goal. Is it merely to get to a certain place, or is the drive itself the

The road trip you take with your kids today may be the one they remember when they look back on their own favorite vacations.

children, to stop at historic landmarks and scenic overlooks, they, too, will develop a lasting appreciation for the area through which they're riding.

Stopping anywhere, of course, is good, because sitting in a car shouldn't be akin to medieval torture. To head off the

vacation? Even families who have a particular destination to reach may want to allow extra time to make the drive more enjoyable. If you arrive at your hotel or your parents' house after a marathon 14 hours in the car, it's unlikely you'll enjoy much of the first day there.

If driving is the vacation, plan an itinerary that allows you to take your time and doesn't require day after day of long hours at the wheel. You're in charge—you're not at the mercy of an airline or rail schedule. In between food and rest stops, give children a chance to enjoy the experience. Let them help navigate—their eyes are probably better than yours for reading those tiny route numbers on road maps anyway. Ask them to search for signs when you aren't sure where you're going. Have them read the campground directory and pick a place to stop for the night.

When everyone starts to get tired and irritable, however, forget family bonding and call for some quiet time. Children can listen to their CD or cassette players (headphones required), read or work on an activity book, or close their eyes and rest. Or you might try listening to an audio book that everyone will enjoy.

ALONG THE RAILS

Trains, too, give you a sense of the land. You can't stop when something really piques your interest, as you can in a car, but train tracks often run through remote and scenic areas where no highways go. In those places, your view is not interrupted by pavement and you're not surrounded by hundreds of other vehicles.

The many restored and refurbished trains throughout the United States are a special treat for families. As an alternative to long-distance passenger service, there are steam engines, cog railways, incline railways, and narrow-gauge railways, each offering a unique travel experience.

Trains are less confining than automobiles, and they come equipped with bathrooms and snack bars, and often have dining and sleeping cars. On a train, you won't have to worry about cabin pressure or canceling a trip because your child gets an ear infection at the last minute. Best of all, you're not driving. Train travel offers an interlude in busy lives when there's absolutely nothing required of you but sitting, looking, talking, playing, and enjoying.

Unfortunately, trains can be expensive. And they are not the place to try to save major bucks. Don't even consider an overnight train trip unless you're able and willing to pay for a sleeping berth or compartment. If you're riding in a public coach car, trying to get your kids to sleep through the night in their seats will be almost impossible. When you consider the train trip itself an important part of your vacation experience, it makes sense to spend a little more money to make that experience a pleasant one.

Room to Move

Try not to ask kids to go from one confined space (a car) to another (a sit-down restaurant) when traveling. Instead, choose a picnic area, a restaurant with outdoor seating or play spaces, or a family restaurant where no one will mind if kids constantly get up and down.

The huff and puff *of an old-fashioned steam train is compelling for toddlers and older kids alike. They'll learn a lot about history and the landscape, even on a short trip.*

You can save *some* money on a train. Pack your own snacks and drinks—even dinner if you can manage it. Train food is expensive and not always tasty. Still, sitting in the dining car with white tablecloths and napkins while the world flies by is something a child will long remember.

If you do get sleeping berths, ask for those in the newer cars that don't require that you lift up the entire lower berth in order to use the toilet. In the middle of the night, that's a real inconvenience.

Children differ dramatically in their tolerance for sitting still, their need to walk and wriggle, and their patience. If you have children age six or younger, think carefully before booking a multiday excursion. In general, a 24-hour train trip is all right for families with small children.

A word about logistics: Some stations don't have baggage handlers to help you.

And in big cities, the stations often have many stairs. When you make your reservations, ask for specifics about the stations you'll be using. If there are lots of stairs, you may want to bring backpacks rather than wheeled luggage. If you don't have lots of bags but you have an infant or toddler, you may want to put your child in a backpack rather than a stroller. The more questions you ask, the better your chances of choosing the right luggage and the right equipment for your journey.

Sitting in the dining car while the world flies by is something a child will remember long into adulthood.

For those traveling abroad, trains can be the best way to go. European trains are often economical, even if you go first class. And now with superspeed trains in various parts of the world, train travel can be as speedy as air travel when you factor in time you'd spend getting to the airport.

KEEPING KIDS HAPPY

———— ✳ ————

A S HARD AS IT MAY SEEM, IT IS POSSIBLE TO KEEP KIDS CONTENT ON A LONG JOURNEY. YOU SIMPLY NEED TO PAY ATTENTION TO TWO MAIN COMPONENTS: THEIR PHYSICAL COMFORT AND THEIR MENTAL STIMULATION.

Nothing beats a trip with kids who are happy and engaged with their surroundings. But few things are worse than when boredom or discomfort starts endless rounds of "Are we there yet?"

SIMPLE COMFORTS

Physical comfort is pretty basic. Kids, like most other people, don't want to be too hot, cold, wet, or crowded. Parents should try to regulate the temperature whenever possible. When the environment is out of your control, as it is on planes, trains, and boats, make adjustments to your children's clothing—take some off, put some on—or use blankets.

If you're traveling with children in diapers, you'll need to change them far more frequently than you do at home.

You'll have limited outfits on hand, so the goal is to change babies *before* they get soaked. Build frequent stops into your driving schedule, and pull over to the side of the road every time your baby is even the slightest bit wet.

On airplanes, use the lavatory for changing diapers; flight attendants frown on parents changing their baby on airplane seats. When there's no option, be discreet. If you change your baby in the seat, put the dirty diaper in a bag (such as those for airsickness) and take it immediately to the lavatory for disposal.

MIND GAMES

Your children's interests and personalities will dictate the activities that will keep them happy and engaged while traveling.

An old-fashioned sing-along
is just the thing for a long car trip.

Crowd Pleasers

Before you go, stock up on a selection of inexpensive finger puzzles, games, or small toys. Each day you're on the road, dole out one to each child as a reward for good behavior the day before. You'll be surprised at how well this simple diversion helps to keep the peace.

Books and maps are time-honored antidotes for boredom. For example, many publishing companies make atlases and geography-oriented activity books. Some of them include information about specific areas—cities, states and provinces, and parks, for example—so find the books that cover places you are traveling through or to. Activity books often have spaces to fill in information about your destination and suggestions for pastimes and games while you travel.

There are guidebooks specifically aimed at children, too. Let your children read these books and tell *you* something about the places you're visiting. If they show an interest in a particular sight to see, do your best to stop there.

Read and research on your own ahead of time so you can periodically bring up an interesting fact or start a discussion. If you're a member of the AAA or CAA and are traveling with one of their TripTiks (customized strip maps that guide you from one point to another), you'll usually

be able to find fascinating facts about each stretch of road, such as what's likely to be growing in those fields you're passing.

If you're interested in what you're seeing, your kids will be, too. Travelers in the western United States can search for sites along the Oregon Trail or where Lewis and Clark ventured. Sites of historic battles or natural disasters are also interesting. Sometimes just by stopping briefly at a visitor center, you can get enough brochures to keep kids occupied for a whole day. Your destinations don't have to be famous. All kinds of sites can fascinate children: locks, dams, hatcheries, waterfalls, construction projects, ponds, parks, trails, fountains, and outdoor sculptures. Take a break from the road and give your kids something new to think about.

Keeping a journal—whether written or drawn—is great for children who really

What a thrill! *For many kids, the chance to see wildlife up-close-and-personal is the highlight of the vacation. So if you happen upon a natural drama, pull over for a photo.*

want to. It's OK to remind gently, but if it turns into a battle of wills, the point will be lost. Sometimes by offering to help, or by making journal time a one-on-one activity with you, you can encourage even reluctant chroniclers to keep going.

TRAVEL TOYS

There are hundreds of commercial games and activities that lend themselves well to travel, and some are even designed specifically for travel. Among them: magnetic versions of family favorites, such as checkers and chess; magnetic boards on which you design pictures with magnetic shapes; washable markers for artwork; sets of crayons and colored pencils, too. (See the checklist on page 132.)

Vinyl stickers are ideal for train and car windows and for airplane tray tables, and reusable stickers of all kinds can be stuck and unstuck to paper, coloring books, and activity books. Some travel kits include stickers, crayons, and more. Books on tape are good for very young children using a tape player; they can follow along in a book even if they can't read. Trivia games are also terrific for children and parents to play together.

Sometimes, though, the road itself provides an activity. In rural areas, you can count how many different ways farmers stack hay, or you can tally the number of horses, dogs, sheep, cows, cats, white cars, or red trucks you pass. And don't forget childhood favorites: I Spy, Geography, 20 Questions. These games challenge generation after generation and can be played just about anywhere.

KEEP YOUNG CHILDREN ENTERTAINED AND YOU'LL FIND THAT THEY MAKE BETTER TRAVEL COMPANIONS.

Travel activity books
With pages for reading, answering questions, and playing games, these books keep kids occupied and teach them about the world.

Magnetic boards
Magnetic boards for puzzles or games are great for travel, since pieces don't get jostled when you turn corners or stop suddenly.

Tape players
A book-and-tape set lets kids follow a story even if they can't read. Some have microphones for recording travel narratives.

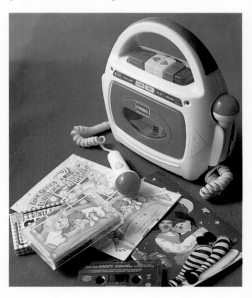

COPING WHEN TRAVEL GETS TRYING

---— ✳ ———

WHAT ARE THE ODDS THAT EVERYTHING WILL GO OFF WITHOUT A HITCH ON YOUR NEXT FAMILY VACATION? LIKE IT OR NOT, CHANCES ARE THAT SOMETHING, SOMEWHERE ALONG THE LINE, WILL PROBABLY GO WRONG.

And that's why traveling in general, and traveling with kids in particular, requires one nonnegotiable, all-important, absolute must-have attitude adjustment: a finely tuned sense of humor.

Your best bet as a traveling parent is to go with the flow—and expect some rapids. That way, if all goes well, you'll be pleasantly surprised. And when something does go awry, you'll handle it. Because it's how you view those rapids that frequently determines whether you have a full-blown disaster on your hands, or just a minor

cyberspace, leaving your three-year-old with a seat 10 rows behind you; you might miss your connecting flight by five minutes or five hours; your kids' meals might get diverted to another plane; a crew member could have an emergency, leaving you stuck at the gate until a replacement can arrive; the flight attendant could run out of the one type of meal anyone in your family would actually eat; you might get bumped off an oversold flight because you didn't get to the airport on time. For any number of reasons, you could end up

Your best bet as a traveling parent is to go with the flow—and expect some rapids. That way, if all goes well, you'll be pleasantly surprised.

setback. You can be almost sure, too, that whatever attitude you adopt, your children will adopt as well. If you respond to snags with anger and frustration, multiply it by the number of people in your family and you'll quickly see where that leads.

Here are some of the things that can —and do—go wrong on vacations: Your luggage could visit Cancún while you visit California; your flight could be canceled because of poor weather or faulty equipment; your seat selections might be lost in

spending long hours, or days, waiting in the airport, sleeping on benches, watching your supply of formula dwindle, spending your vacation cash on expensive airport meals, and wondering if your flight is ever going to get off the ground.

They won't *all* happen on your trip, but these are real possibilities that have befallen real families—more than once. They are also things over which you have absolutely no control. So prepare for the worst, and hope for the best. However justified your wrath may be, it will do you no good in dealing with unforeseen set-backs. But it will leave you feeling more stressed out than ever. So instead of losing it, try these five stress-busting techniques:

◆ THINK OF WAYS TO KEEP PROBLEMS FROM ARISING IN THE FIRST PLACE.

◆ MAINTAIN YOUR SENSE OF HUMOR—GETTING MAD WILL JUST MAKE THINGS WORSE.

◆ AIM TO STAY CALM AND TO SPEAK IN A CALM VOICE.

◆ BE PERSISTENT ABOUT ASKING FOR WHAT YOU WANT.

◆ TREAT TRAVEL SNAFUS AS PART OF THE ADVENTURE.

A positive attitude and a sense of humor will always help you de-stress and make your kids feel better even when life is a hassle. Sometimes, these attributes may even be the key to success—that ticket agent may be inspired to go the extra mile to help if you respond to a bad situation with humor and a good attitude.

BE PREPARED

At other times the solution may not come so easily. Which is why beating problems to the punch and being prepared may be the most important technique of all. Basic measures include packing extra clothes, diapers, snacks, and other essentials in your carry-on. You should also make sure that you bring along enough books, tapes, and other activities for you and your kids to make it through a long wait, whether it's the result of a missed or cancelled flight or a major car problem.

Always carry a guidebook so that you can find something fun to do if it turns out you have a day to kill en route. Also,

Change of plans? *Was the museum closed? Did you miss the ferry? An emergency supply of books, games, and coloring books can keep kids entertained back at the hotel.*

you should have enough cash or credit on your credit card to get a hotel room or rent a car if necessary.

Look for creative alternatives when your best-laid plans go wrong. You might, for example, consider flying to a city that's near where your missed flight was headed, renting a car there, and driving the rest of the way. You should also consider having an emergency road-assistance plan so that you don't use your vacation funds paying for a tow-truck driver and a mechanic.

Finally, don't underestimate the importance of getting to the airport long before the mandatory arrival time. If you are among the first passengers to learn your flight has been canceled, you may have a better shot of getting on the next flight than someone who shows up 10 minutes before the scheduled departure.

Keeping the Vacation Spirit

---- ✳ ----

ALL GOOD THINGS, INCLUDING VACATIONS, MUST COME TO AN END. YOU CAN'T DO ANYTHING ABOUT THAT, BUT YOU CAN MAKE THE ENDING A HAPPY ONE, AND CARRY THOSE POSITIVE FEELINGS INTO YOUR HOME LIFE.

Try to make the last day of your vacation unhurried. Pack the night before if you can, and leave as much of the day as possible unscheduled and utterly relaxed. Sleep in, have a late breakfast, or do nothing but loll around the pool. Take a final ski run on an easy slope with the whole family—even the little ones, if they're up for it. Stroll, putter, dawdle—do anything but rush. Save one last lazy activity for this day: a paddle out on the lake, a carriage ride, a bike trip around town.

When you finally head for the train station or airport, leave yourselves plenty of time to get there without rushing or worrying. When you determine how much time that is, tack on an additional 30 minutes to account for random family mishaps. If you're traveling by car, leave enough time so you won't feel as if you're in a race to get home.

Try to schedule travel so that you don't arrive home late at night. If you get back in the afternoon or early evening, you can even relax before bedtime. Finish the last chapter of that potboiler beach novel, pick up the telephone and catch up with friends, or just lie around as a family and reflect on your adventure.

Ski one more great trail *with the whole family or linger over breakfast on your last day before packing up and hitting the road.*

Children, since they live in the moment, have an easier time of staying in vacation mode. Adults, however, live mostly in the future. They have to think ahead about what must be done and how to do it—and after a vacation there's a lot to think

Your vacation isn't over until you hit the morning rush hour, so enjoy it until the very end.

about. Adults often find themselves back at work, at least in their minds, before they ever leave the hotel or cottage. If you find yourself mentally preparing for that first meeting or worrying about the backlog of papers awaiting you at the office, force yourself to stop. Your vacation isn't over until you hit the morning rush hour, so enjoy it until the very end.

In order to stay relaxed longer, make sure you've scheduled your vacation so that you have a free day, or at least a half day, at home at the end of your trip. You'll still have chores to do—unpacking, opening mail, picking up pets—but you'll have the necessary time in which to do them. That way, you can avoid the frenetic, frazzled feeling that seems to wipe out in a second all the benefits of your vacation. You might even consider sleeping late the morning after you get home, which is a luxury not to be underestimated.

Vacation is a way in which families get closer, enjoy each other, maybe even see each other in an entirely new light. Vacations make you feel good, which is a feeling that's well worth preserving. Then,

The bond between siblings *is often strengthened by the adventures they've been able to share on a vacation.*

perhaps, the next time your son tracks mud all over the living room carpet, you can manage not to live in *that* moment, but concentrate on the memories of crashing waves, salty sea air, and the adventures you've shared as a family.

The Road Home

Getting there may be half the fun, but don't abandon the spirit of adventure on the way home, either. Schedule enough travel time so you don't have to rush back. Then, just as you did on the way there, stop whenever a sight along the way piques your interest.

HEALTH and
Safety TIPS

—✳—

1 Ask your insurance providers about your **coverage** in case of illness, injury, or items stolen while traveling. **2** Carry a **first-aid kit** with essentials customized for your destination. **3** Keep needed **medications with you** in case checked luggage goes astray. **4** If you're visiting grandparents, ask them to move medications **out of the reach** of babies and toddlers. **5** When you arrive at your destination, teach children the **number** of your room, cottage, condo, or campsite. **6** Check your accommodations thoroughly and **childproof** as necessary. **7** Teach children **never to open** hotel doors to anyone unless they know it's you or another trusted person. **8** When sightseeing in crowded areas, prearrange a **place to meet** if someone gets lost. **9** When hiking or camping, have children wear a **whistle** in case they wander away. **10** Be aware that foreign medications may contain **aspirin,** which children would not be given at home. ●

STAYING SAFE AND WELL

A SURVIVOR'S GUIDE TO VACATIONS

* —— * —— *

Keeping your family healthy and safe on the road is a matter of two different but equally important strategies: taking preventive measures and knowing what to do in case of a sudden illness or other emergency.

While there are many ailments, minor injuries, and safety concerns that could arise when traveling with children, the good news is that you, as a parent, already know how to handle most of them yourself. Most of the rest require only common sense and some thoughtful planning and packing.

It goes without saying that prevention is the best route, so pay particular attention to what you can do before you leave home and each time you head out on a vacation adventure. Having the right clothing, supplies, and safety gear is considerably easier and cheaper than finding unfamiliar doctors and paying medical bills in the middle of a foreign country— especially if your credit cards or passports are lost or stolen.

AN OUNCE OF PREVENTION

✳

JUST BECAUSE YOUR FAMILY IS FULLY PROTECTED BY HEALTH INSURANCE AT HOME DOESN'T NECESSARILY MEAN THAT THE SAME TYPE OR EXTENT OF COVERAGE WILL FOLLOW YOU ON VACATION.

So as you plan your travels, call your provider to find out about coverage while you are away. Here are questions to ask:

◆ ARE WE COVERED IN OTHER REGIONS, STATES, AND COUNTRIES?

◆ DOES COVERAGE INCLUDE ROUTINE ILLNESSES OR JUST EMERGENCY CARE?

◆ MUST WE USE CERTAIN DOCTORS AND FACILITIES, OR CAN WE CHOOSE?

◆ MUST WE GET YOUR APPROVAL BEFORE SEEKING CARE?

◆ ARE WE COVERED FOR AMBULANCE TRANSPORTATION?

◆ DO WE MAKE CO-PAYMENTS, OR MUST WE PAY IN FULL AND BE REIMBURSED?

The answers to these questions will help you decide how to proceed in the event

Rx to Go

Heading out of the country or far from medical facilities? Ask your pediatrician for an oral antibiotic to take along for infections or other nonemergency bacterial illnesses. For babies and young children, get a powder to mix with bottled water if and when you need it. Try chewables for older kids.

of illness or emergency, and whether you may need to purchase supplemental coverage from another source. If your insurance provider does cover you outside your area, have the company send you a list of affiliated facilities or physicians, as well as its brochure on out-of-area care. Read the material carefully; if there's anything you don't understand, call the company to get clarification before you leave home. And always carry each family member's insurance card with you when you travel.

Medical emergencies are also covered under most travel insurance policies, which give you another reason to buy this extra protection. If you must interrupt your trip because of illness, the policy will cover lost deposits or other expenses. Some policies pay for medical expenses for up to a year if the initial treatment occurred during the insured trip. Emergency dental care may also be provided under these policies.

You should also check your credit card for medical benefits. Some will provide emergency airlifting—highly expensive if you are not covered—and medical aid in foreign destinations. Some will get medication delivered to you wherever you may be. Read the fine print in your credit card information, or call customer service and arrange to have written information sent to you before you leave.

WHEREVER YOU GO

Whether you're traveling by car, airplane, bus, or train, carry a first-aid kit with you. There are basic products families should always have (see suggestions at right), but you should also customize your kit to your destination. If you're going hiking, for example, carry a lotion such as calamine that relieves rashes and insect bites. If your hike is going to be lengthy and you don't normally spend all day on your feet, bring plenty of moleskin and assume you'll have blisters to soothe.

It's a good idea to call the hotels and resorts where you'll be staying to find out if there's a doctor or nurse on call. Club Med family resorts, for example, routinely have one or both. Ask what these practitioners charge and whether you can bill the service to your room or must pay for it separately. If the latter, you may want to bring extra cash, as some doctors in remote areas don't take credit cards or checks.

Most cruise lines will have a doctor on board, and some even dispense medication for motion sickness at no charge. Ask if they do and whether the medicine will be safe for your child. If not, bring your own motion-sickness medication.

Families heading into the wilderness need to take extra precautions because emergency help can be a long time arriving. One of the advantages of going with a guide is that most have been trained in wilderness first aid and carry equipment to safeguard families and to contact medical help should an emergency arise. Ask guides ahead of time about their training and whether they'll have two-way radios.

WHETHER YOU'RE HEADED FOR A BIG CITY OR A CAMPSITE, BE SURE TO TAKE ALONG A WELL-STOCKED FIRST-AID KIT.

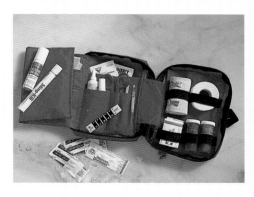

For cuts, scrapes, and blisters

You need alcohol wipes or antiseptic towelettes, antibiotic ointment, an assortment of adhesive bandages (if kids like cartoon characters or colors, get those), and sterile pads. If you'll be hiking or participating in any other sport that could bring on blisters, take along some moleskin.

For bites, stings, and rashes

Bring ointment, lotion, or stick for insect-sting relief; an anti-itch medication (which may be an analgesic, an antihistamine, or a combination of both); tweezers to remove ticks; and a cold compress to make stings feel better and reduce swelling. If anyone in your family is allergic to bee stings, also bring along a prescription bee-sting kit for immediate treatment.

Miscellaneous items

A thermometer is a must. Those that go in the ear are quick and can be used anywhere, even on an airplane. Temperature-sensing strips, though less accurate, are lightweight and portable, convenient for backpacking. Gauze or cotton balls are useful for a variety of minor injuries and irritations; small scissors come in handy for cutting moleskin, bandages, or gauze. And don't forget a bag or pouch in which to carry everything.

Easy Does It

If you must use insect repellent on your child's skin, choose one with no more than 10 percent DEET (the active ingredient). In higher concentrations, DEET can be dangerous for children.

If the guide sounds uncertain about how to handle emergencies or has too casual an attitude ("We've never had a problem, so don't worry"), find another guide. Also ask how far the nearest medical facility will be and whether it is equipped to handle pediatric emergencies.

Do keep in mind, too, that some outdoor trips are good for families precisely because they don't take you too far from civilization. Many outfitters offer adventures in rafting, hiking, canoeing, sailing, and rock climbing, among others, all in

will be—the trails you'll be hiking on, the campsites you're headed for, the stretch of river or the lake you'll be on. And always check in with local rangers to give them your itinerary and timetable. Let rangers know that you'll stop back on your way out so that if you're delayed, they'll know to start looking for you. Never head into the wilderness—not even on a day hike—without a flashlight, extra clothing, water, food, matches, and rain gear.

Because ticks and other biting insects share the outdoor world with you, you should take preventive measures whenever you're hiking, camping, or exploring open spaces. The best prevention against ticks is to wear long pants, long socks, closed shoes, a long-sleeved shirt, and a hat. This happens to be good protection against sunburn and poisonous plants, too, so you can take care of three worries with one outfit. If it's hot, the clothing should be made of cotton or other lightweight, breathable fabric; if the garments are light colored,

Families venturing alone into the wild should take a first-aid kit and a two-way radio. At least one parent should know CPR.

the great outdoors but still near medical help. If you have a young child or a family member with a chronic illness, you might want to try one of these trips.

Families venturing alone into the wild should be sure to take a first-aid kit (see page 85) and a two-way radio to contact the outside world. At least one of the parents should have certification in cardiopulmonary resuscitation (CPR). Also let someone at home know exactly where you

ticks are easier to find. Insect repellents can also help, but use them carefully. Ask your pediatrician about repellents for very young children, and whether to select those that go directly on the skin or those for use on the outside of clothing.

Remember that the notorious Lyme-disease-carrying deer tick is often no bigger than the head of a pin. After you leave the woods or fields, check children and adults thoroughly for ticks; also check pets if you have them with you. If you know you'll be hiking or camping in areas where poison ivy, poison oak, or poison sumac is rampant, wear long pants and long-sleeved shirts and ask your doctor or pharmacist about preventive lotions. If you've come in contact with the plants (or with pets who have brushed against them), thoroughly wash your skin with soap and cold water to prevent or limit the spread of the rash. Wash clothing, too, and bathe any pets whose fur has touched the vegetation.

MEDICATIONS

Prevention is crucial when you travel to other countries, because you and your children will be exposed to a new population of disease-causing agents against which you may have no immunity. Some, such as certain strains of malaria, are especially dangerous for children; others can cause fatal illnesses in children and adults. Several weeks before you leave, check with the travel department of your health-care

provider or call a travel clinic (see page 143 for resources) to determine which medications and immunizations you and your children need. Be aware that some countries also require you to prove that you've been inoculated against certain diseases, so check specific entry requirements well in advance of your departure date.

If family members are on prescription medicines, pack an extra copy of each prescription, along with your doctors' and pharmacist's phone numbers, in case you need to call for a refill. Never pack prescription medication in checked luggage, and if you're traveling out of the country, keep all medications in their original containers so customs or border officials can see exactly what they are.

As you decide what medications to bring, remember that it's not always easy to find children's over-the-counter (OTC) drugs when you're traveling, especially in airports, hotels, train stations, small communities, and foreign countries. Here are

First-aid supplies should be on everybody's packing list.

some of the children's OTC remedies and medications you might need to carry with you; check with your pediatrician about brands and dosages suitable for your kids:

◆ NONASPIRIN PAIN RELIEVER

◆ DECONGESTANT

◆ ANTIDIARRHEA MEDICATION

◆ MOTION-SICKNESS MEDICATION

◆ COUGH MEDICINE (EXPECTORANT, SUPPRESSANT, OR BOTH)

◆ ANTIHISTAMINE

For all other general medications and first-aid supplies, stock up on generic brands at discount stores before you leave—it'll save money and worry if you're traveling where such necessities aren't readily available.

Families visiting relatives should be aware that grandparents' medications pose a danger for very young children. Your parents and in-laws are no longer used to having small children around; they may leave pills out on nightstands or counters, and they may not use childproof containers. Unfortunately, some pills look like candy to toddlers. Before arriving, call and remind grandparents to put medications out of sight and reach. Also let them know that you'll be bringing along childproofing equipment so you can secure one or two rooms for your toddler.

SUN PROTECTION

One of the primary health concerns for vacationing parents and children is sunburn. Whether you're going to the beach or the mountains, whether it's summer or winter, sunscreen is imperative. Use a product with a sun protection factor (SPF) of at least 15 (look for products that have a seal of approval from the Skin Cancer Foundation). It's important to reapply sunscreen frequently, even if the package claims the product is sweat- or waterproof, and to continue using it when you're in the shade, because sun reflects

Apply sunscreen often *when kids visit the beach. Research has shown that children who are repeatedly sunburned have a higher incidence of skin cancer as adults.*

off water and sand. Also reapply sunscreen more often when you're skiing; snow reflects sunlight, and the thinner air of high altitudes filters out fewer rays. The sun is most dangerous between 10 A.M. and 3 P.M. in middle latitudes; near the equator the danger period is longer. For additional protection, schedule outdoor activities for the morning and late afternoon hours and save museum visits for midday.

Doctors strongly advise that babies not be in the sun at all; if they must go outdoors, dress them in long-sleeved shirts and long pants—preferably cotton, which is more breathable than synthetics.

so they can participate; children are usually welcome as long as they're with a parent. You can teach your little ones stretches or floor exercises, which will go faster and be more fun if you're doing them together. A jump rope is easy to pack and offers great exercise for children and adults. Biking and swimming also give excellent workouts, and many popular vacation spots will give you access to one or both.

As for eating on the road, you can keep healthful habits while still indulging a little. Try not to give into kids' requests to eat at fast-food joints while you're driving. Look for interesting local restaurants where

Invite your children to share a fitness regimen with you, whether it's jogging along the beach or power walking around the campground.

And don't forget a hat; hats with brims all the way around are better than baseball caps for all ages. If kids start to show signs of burning, go inside immediately. Once burning occurs, no amount of sunscreen will protect your child's skin.

Someone may end up with a burn in spite of your precautions, so always carry aloe gel or other burn-relief lotion. Then have that person stay out of the sun.

STAYING IN SHAPE

Going on vacation does not mean that you have to give up on regular fitness routines or that you're doomed to gain 10 pounds while away. Invite your children to share a fitness regimen with you, whether it's jogging along the beach or power walking around the campground. Bring them along to your hotel's or cruise ship's fitness center

you can try regional cuisine while avoiding high-fat, high-salt foods. Eat one or two lighter-than-normal meals every day, especially if you're on a cruise or at an all-inclusive resort where food is plentiful. That way you won't feel guilty when you do indulge. Shop for the same foods you eat at home; salads and grilled meats can make an easy, healthful vacation dinner if you're in a cottage or a condo and cooking on your own. Remember that if everyone's swimming, hiking, or otherwise burning plenty of calories, you'll need energy-building meals and snacks, not junk foods.

And if you go crazy occasionally—when the hotel chef makes three luscious chocolate desserts and you just have to try them all—don't be too hard on yourself. You're on vacation! You can always get back on track the next day.

MOMMY, MY HEAD HURTS!

---✳---

EVEN WITH GOOD PLANNING, KIDS DO GET SICK ON VACATION. SOMETIMES TRAVEL ITSELF CAUSES DISCOMFORT. THANKFULLY, MOST TRAVEL-RELATED AILMENTS CAN BE TREATED WITH OTC MEDICATIONS AND SOME COMMON SENSE.

The primary travel-induced discomforts for children are ear or sinus pain brought on by pressure changes in airplanes, and motion sickness, which commonly affects travelers in cars and on boats but can also occur while in an airplane.

When you fly, bring a children's pain reliever and decongestant. If you know your child suffers from ear pain during airplane trips, ask your pediatrician about giving a dose of decongestant during travel as a preventive measure. Nursing or giving a bottle to babies and young children during takeoff and landing can help relieve ear pressure; older kids can try chewing

gum. In addition, there are products available, such as disposable ear plugs, that will help reduce flight-related pain.

If motion sickness is a problem for your kids, talk to your pediatrician about the right medication and dosage for them. Some motion-sickness medications make kids groggy, which isn't necessarily bad, but you could end up carrying sleeping children through airports or into hotels. During car travel, eat light meals and offer snacks such as crackers and ginger ale, which can help settle upset stomachs. On a boat, have your child sit topside if possible; being in the open and able to see the horizon can help seasick kids feel better.

There are many suggestions for overcoming jet lag; most suggest that travelers of all ages do better with plenty of rest before and during travel. As for sleeping and eating schedules in the new time zone, there are differing points of view. Ask your pediatrician or travel clinic for recommendations. Most experts agree that eating meals high in protein and low in fat before and during travel can help to ease jet lag. In general, children adjust to time changes more quickly than their parents do, so don't be too concerned about this.

What is a big concern in some foreign destinations is diarrhea—especially for very young children and elderly travelers.

The View From Here

Children prone to car sickness do better if they can look out a window and see the horizon. Make sure car seats put them up high enough for that. Older children do better up front; if that's not safe (in cars with passenger-side air bags), make sure they can at least see out. Fresh air also helps, so open a window if it's not too cold.

Getting sick on vacation is no fun. Prevention is the best medicine.

Talk to your pediatrician about preventive medications such as daily doses of an OTC upset-stomach remedy for adults and children. The primary preventive strategy, however, is to avoid local water and ice cubes, including those served in hotels and restaurants; to brush your teeth with bottled water; to eat well-cooked foods; and to avoid any fruits and vegetables that have not been cooked except those you wash (with bottled water) and peel yourself. If you will be far from medical help or in an area with questionable medical care, ask your doctor for an antibiotic to have on hand in case of severe or ongoing diarrhea.

High altitude affects some adults and children more than others. Symptoms include headaches, dizziness, and nausea. The first course of action is to limit activities for a day or two after you arrive. And because the air is thinner at high altitudes, you breathe more frequently and thus lose more water as you exhale—so drink a lot more water than you think you need.

Children don't usually drink unless they're thirsty, so you'll have to keep track to make sure everyone gets six to eight glasses of water a day. A high-carbohydrate, low-protein diet may help prevent or relieve altitude sickness. Avoiding salt and salty foods can help as well.

When it comes to insect bites, prevention is the best medicine (see page 85). If your kids do get bitten or stung, apply an antiseptic and a pain-relief ointment; an antihistamine will relieve the related itching and swelling. Remove ticks carefully with tweezers; don't hold a match to them in the hope they'll pull out on their own; this is dangerous and unproductive. If your family visits an area where deer ticks are prevalent—even if you never see a tick —watch for later signs of a rash or symptoms of the flu, which could mean Lyme disease. Untreated, Lyme disease is serious.

Keep young kids shaded *to prevent sunburn. Dress them in long pants, long-sleeved shirts, and hats with full brims.*

Safeguarding People and Property

---　✳　---

Thinking ahead is the best way to ensure safety during vacation. It's especially important to give children the information they'll need in case of an emergency—such as if they get separated from you.

How much information you give and how detailed your contingency plans are will depend on the ages of your children.

DURING TRAVEL

Keep your family safe by using seat belts and child safety seats. Whenever your car is in motion or you're seated in an airplane, seat belts should be worn. Period. If you have to nurse your baby, attend to a crying child in the backseat, get something you can't reach from your seat, or make a snack, pull over and stop the car. If you have to use lavatories on an airplane or get up and walk with an antsy child, by all means do that if the seat-belt sign is off. But small children are especially vulnerable to injury if they are unrestrained during turbulence. The best routine is for kids and adults to keep seat belts at least loosely fastened when seated in a plane.

In cars, the safest place for your children is in the rear seat. Occasionally, kids can sit in the front—unless your car is equipped with a passenger-side air bag.

> **When your car is in motion, seat belts should be worn. Period. The safest place for your children is in the rear seat.**

Research has shown that air bags can be deadly for any child under the age of 12 and even for a small, lightweight adult. Unless your car has an on-off switch for the air bag (or until cars come equipped with child-safe air bags), do not let kids ride in the front seat. If you are visiting grandparents and you're unsure about their vehicles, ask. Let grandparents know if kids may sit in front, and emphasize that they must always be in seat belts or car seats. In the United States, kids age 4 and younger and/or weighing 40 pounds (18kg) or less should always ride in car seats.

In addition to safeguarding children, parents must also safeguard money and

Heads Up

Put a chair by your hotel or condo door so kids can see out of the peephole. That way they can make certain it's you—or someone they know and trust—before they open up.

travel documents. Keeping track of these is hard enough when you're traveling with adults, let alone when you're distracted by children. Put money and documents where you won't need to watch them, such as in a travel wallet in your carry-on luggage or glove compartment, or in a money belt.

AT YOUR DESTINATION

As soon as you arrive and get settled, make sure children know the number of your hotel room, cottage, condo, or campsite. Take kids on a short tour of the area so they know how to get back to your home base. Teach older children how to call the registration desk, and show them where it's located. If your children aren't used to elevators, show them the button to push for your rooms and for the lobby area; explain about the emergency button, but make certain they know it's only for emergencies. Teach kids never to open your hotel door to strangers.

Parents should also check accommodations for potential safety problems. Run hot water and feel it. If it's scalding hot, don't let very young kids run their own bath. Look to see if there's any way a child could leave without your knowing. If your lodging includes a full kitchen, check for sharp utensils in reachable drawers and move them to safer locations. If there is a potentially dangerous object—such as a knife block or a heavy jar—that a child could pull down from a countertop, move the item out of harm's way. If the stove or oven has dials that a toddler can reach, remove the dials and replace them only when you are using the stove.

KEEP YOUR CHILDREN AND YOUR BELONGINGS SAFE WITH THESE HANDY TAKE-ALONG ITEMS.

Luggage locks

Use luggage locks on suitcases you check. Combination locks like this one are a better choice than key locks, which are easy to pry open and whose keys are easy to lose. Bring extras along in case your vacation purchases necessitate checking a bag you didn't check before. You can also use these locks to secure luggage in your hotel room, though a hotel's safe is a better place to keep your valuables.

ID bracelets

If you have young children who could wander off and be uncertain how to find you, have them wear an ID bracelet—such as this disposable band that can be secured around a child's wrist. Pertinent information—your child's name and where you're staying—is concealed on the underside of the bracelet, where authorities can find it if they need to.

KIDPROOFING A HOTEL ROOM

⁕

THE SAME THINGS THAT ARE hazards to your children at home are dangerous in hotels and vacation condos. Make childproofing accessories part of your travel kit, and install the appropriate safety devices as soon as you arrive. Don't forget to take them when you leave. For a childproofing checklist, see page 133.

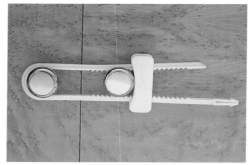

Cabinet locks *keep dangerous items securely out of reach and prevent children from opening doors that can pinch their fingers.*

Inflatable faucet covers *are easy to pack. They prevent serious head and face injuries to babies and toddlers in the tub.*

A night-light *illuminates the way to a bathroom or parent when a child wakes up in unfamiliar surroundings.*

Plug-in covers *keep curious toddlers from probing electric outlets. Carry enough of these to childproof several outlets.*

If you have a baby or a toddler, be even more thorough. Things to look for: sharp corners on coffee tables, breakable glassware, matches, exposed outlets, coffeepots that could be pulled down, cabinets that could pinch fingers, windows and sliding-glass doors that open and don't have bars, balconies with spaces in the railings large enough for young children to fit through, or furniture they might climb on to reach high objects or the tops of railings.

When part of your vacation involves being in crowded, unfamiliar areas, families should have a prearranged meeting spot in case anyone gets lost. If you're in a theme park, aquarium, or zoo, for example, arrange to meet by the entrance gate or at the door of a particular gift shop. Even with a meeting place, it's a good idea to discuss in advance whom children can go to if they get lost and need help. Security guards and shopkeepers are usually safe bets. When you first arrive, find a park security guard so kids know what the uniforms and badges look like.

If you're sightseeing in town, choose a restaurant or shop to meet in. If children become lost and are unable to locate the meeting place, tell them to ask police or shopkeepers for help. Let them know that it's not a good idea to go up to strangers on the street. Try not to alarm your children as you make your safety plans. Just be matter-of-fact and explain that police officers, store owners, and people who work in parks, museums, train stations, and zoos generally know how to help lost children find their parents quickly.

It's unwise to let kids wear or carry an article of clothing or an accessory with their name on it; it's too easy for strangers to convince children that they're family friends. Some companies make disposable ID bracelets for traveling children (see page 93). When you go out each day, be aware of exactly what your kids are wearing; if you have to describe them to the police or guards, accuracy is important.

IN THE WILD

Camping and learning about outdoor life is an incredible experience for children of all ages. But the wilderness can be a dangerous place—particularly if families are inexperienced or unprepared. Give all kids a whistle to wear. Blowing a whistle takes less energy than yelling and can be heard from farther away. Let the kids know that it's not a toy, and after they blow it a few times because they absolutely can't resist

It's unwise for kids to wear clothing with their name on it; strangers could easily convince children that they're family friends.

doing so, tell them not to blow it again unless they're lost. Remind them of the story about the boy who cried "wolf." In the wilderness, teach kids to stay in one place while they wait for help in case they do get separated from you. This not only makes it easier for rescuers to find them but also prevents possible falls or other injuries that could occur if they were to race around in a panic. Put warm clothes

Stand Out in a Crowd

When sightseeing in crowded places, have each member of your family wear a brightly colored hat—all of them the same hue so you don't have to think about who's wearing what. It can be hard to pick out faces from a distance, especially those of small children standing among tall adults, but a bright hat is easy to spot in a crowd.

and snacks, a flashlight, and a windbreaker or rain gear in kids' day packs, even for short hikes. The brighter the color of the jacket, the easier it will be to spot during a search. Show children how to jump up and down or run in place to stay warm. That way they'll know what to do if the temperature starts to drop. If you will be entering a wilderness area, check with the ranger station to learn if there are any extra precautions you should take regarding local wildlife. Tell children to yell if they hear an animal nearby (the animal will most likely leave) and to answer calls from rescuers even if the voices are unfamiliar. Children have been known to hide from searchers because they feared their parents would be angry at them for getting lost. Let children know that adults can get lost, too, and that you won't be mad at them if they lose their way.

When you're camping, teach children not to run around a campsite—with cook stoves, tent ropes, and campfires, there are too many potential dangers. If you're near water, always use the buddy system both on shore and while kids are swimming, and tell children not to swim unless an adult is near and has checked the water first. And no one should ever dive headfirst into an unfamiliar body of water.

Give kids whistles to blow in case they get separated from you.

EMERGENCIES ABROAD

———— ✳ ————

WHEN TRAVELING IN FOREIGN COUNTRIES, IT'S ESPECIALLY IMPORTANT TO BE WELL ORGANIZED AND PREPARED IN CASE OF AN EMERGENCY. HERE ARE STEPS YOU CAN TAKE TO BE READY FOR A SUDDEN ILLNESS, LOSS, OR THEFT.

If family members do get sick or hurt, be prepared to act quickly. Keep your health insurance provider's 24-hour emergency number handy, and have your insurance ID number ready when you call. Also have your home physician's and pediatrician's numbers in case there are questions about your family's health history.

If your family belongs to the International Association for Medical Assistance to Travellers (see page 143), keep on hand its directory of English-speaking doctors. If you have emergency coverage through your credit card, make sure to take the appropriate 24-hour number with you: the company may be able to give you the names of English-speaking local doctors.

If a foreign physician prescribes medication for your child, check whether it contains aspirin. Because of aspirin's link to Reye's syndrome, a potentially fatal illness, aspirin is not recommended for children under age 19. Also, because of varying national drug-safety standards, you may wish to ask if any medications prescribed for your children abroad are legally permitted for use in your home country.

The loss or theft of passports, credit cards, money, and other valuables can quickly ruin a trip. Use security wallets and hotel safes to protect these items, and don't leave them out in your hotel room.

Two essential phone numbers to take with you at all times are the daytime number of your nearest embassy and, especially if the embassy isn't close, the 24-hour emergency number of your country's nearest diplomatic mission. Get these numbers from your government before you leave. A consular officer can help you transfer money from home and can inform relatives or friends of your plight.

Also have the numbers for reporting lost or stolen credit cards and traveler's checks, including any 24-hour numbers.

The loss of passports, credit cards, money, and other valuables can ruin a trip. Use security wallets and hotel safes to protect these items.

If you've left photocopies of credit cards, tickets, birth certificates, or passports with a friend (see the checklist on page 141 for information to include), carry that friend's phone number. Before calling, ask for a local fax number where copies can be sent, and have ready a number your friend can call to cancel credit cards if necessary.

Finally, families renting cars abroad should carry their automobile insurance company's emergency assistance phone number in case of an accident.

CHOOSING a PLACE
for Everyone

---※---

1 Weigh your primary **lodging needs:** space, privacy, cost, services, atmosphere. **2** If budget is a priority, look for hotels where kids **stay free** in their parents' room. **3** For **multi-generation** vacations, consider cruises with programs for kids and seniors. **4** Keep essential **camping** equipment on hand for spur-of-the-moment family getaways. **5** If you're staying with **relatives,** talk to them in advance about potential problems, such as how to discipline your kids if you aren't there. **6** Use good super-vised **children's programs** to give your kids opportunities for peer interaction and learning. **7** Pay attention to **counselor-to-child ratios** in hotel or cruise programs; too many kids can mean compromised quality. **8** Make vacation **cooking** and meals a time for family fun and togetherness. **9** Make some meals **adults-only time,** because you and your partner need that, too. **10** If cooking is a **hassle** and eating out is too expensive, choose vacation plans that include meals as part of the base price. ●

LODGING
AND DINING

FINDING FAMILY-FRIENDLY ACCOMMODATIONS

* ——— ✳ ——— *

The first decision that most families make when planning a vacation is where to go. That's important, but no more so than finding the right lodging at your destination. No matter how wonderful a locale is, you'll be disappointed if your accommodations don't have what you need.

Then again, no place is perfect for every member of the family, so consider the pros and cons of different types of lodging before you book your vacation. Consider also the services and amenities offered at various lodgings. A high-quality supervised children's program may be central to your plans, but how do you know if a particular program is good? And what about meals? Do you want to eat out every day? Cook? Have someone else take care of cooking altogether?

You have lots of choices when it comes to lodging, services, and food. But once you know what questions to ask and what to look for, making the right choice is simple.

WHERE TO STAY:
FINDING THE RIGHT PLACES

———— ✳ ————

You're lucky to be a traveling parent today; the possibilities of where to stay on your next family-oriented vacation are practically limitless. But therein lies a problem: How do you choose one?

When choosing a place to stay, families weigh amenities, cost, privacy, and space. Here's a breakdown of popular options.

RESORTS AND HOTELS

What makes a hotel or resort family-friendly? Here are things to look for:

- SPECIAL PACKAGES OR PRICES FOR FAMILIES

- A GENERAL ATMOSPHERE THAT SAYS FAMILIES ARE WELCOME

- CHILDREN'S MENUS AND AT LEAST ONE INEXPENSIVE RESTAURANT

- AVAILABLE BABYSITTERS OR A SUPERVISED CHILDREN'S PROGRAM

- ACTIVITIES AIMED AT FAMILIES

- THE AVAILABILITY OF CHILDREN'S VIDEOS AND GAMES

Decide what's most important to you, then ask questions. If you're looking for a good children's program, for example, you'll need a resort with programs that are appropriate to your kids' ages. If you have children under age five, your choices are limited, but there are some programs for preschoolers. A few of the Club Med villages for families accept children at age one or even younger. Some of the great old family resorts—among them the Tyler Place in Vermont—have at least seasonal programs for infants and toddlers.

If budgeting is a priority, book a room in places where children can stay free with parents, but make sure to check the size of the room; some accommodate families better than others. Chain hotels, including Hyatt, will sometimes offer a second room for children at a discount. And some resorts have special prices for children on room or package rates.

It's hard to generalize about resorts because they're so varied, but think about

Where to stay? The options for family vacationers include campsites, hotels, cruise ships, and rustic cabins.

the atmosphere. Many resorts are located in prime tourist areas, and if you want a get-away-from-it-all experience, you'll be disappointed. Likewise, if you want adult nightlife or proximity to off-site attractions, a place in the mountains far from everything is not your best choice. When you choose a resort vacation, you're really choosing the resort itself as opposed to the surrounding area. After all, the resort is where you'll spend most of your time; the quality of that experience is important.

Atmosphere is also important at city hotels and inns, though you may spend less time in them. Still, you'll eat many of your meals and you'll spend each night in your accommodations, so the quality of the room, services, and amenities can affect your vacation, regardless of how much you like the general area.

CRUISES

What's great about a cruise is that you get to see a lot of different places in one trip. Many cruises, especially those in the Caribbean and Hawaii, have excellent children's programs and family activities. Many also have activities aimed at older travelers, which makes a cruise ideal for intergenerational vacations.

Cruises are often best for families who are expecting the shipboard experience itself to be the vacation. If you're hoping to get a real feeling for the ports you visit, you may be disappointed. Check cruise itineraries to see how long you'll be staying in each port, and find out if shipboard programs for kids and adults focus on the culture and people of the various ports.

Cable Caution

In-room movies, provided by cable, can keep kids occupied while parents relax in another room or go to the hotel restaurant for an adult meal. But beware—many systems include R- and X-rated films. Ask the hotel to block access to these movies in your children's rooms.

Programs on ships in Alaska and Hawaii often do, and some of the smaller, more family-friendly vessels in Central America and the Galápagos Islands do, too.

RANCHES AND FARMS

Ranches vary greatly. Some offer infant and toddler care; others don't accept kids under age five. Some focus almost exclusively on riding; at others you can also bike, hike, raft, take seminars, ski, help with chores, round up cattle, or swim and fish to your heart's content. Some ranches have walk-only trail rides, while at others you and your horse can lope across the open spaces. Always ask at what age children can ride out on the trail, whether children and adults can ride in the same groups (at some ranches children ride only in groups with their counselors), and what you can do if your kids are still too young to ride and you want to go on an all-day outing. Don't settle for a ranch that doesn't meet your needs, as there are many others you can choose from.

Farms usually offer a bed-and-breakfast experience. In most cases you and the kids can help with chores, such as feeding or milking the animals. Your experience will vary depending on the season. Spring is an especially good time to visit a working farm because baby animals are plentiful.

FAMILY CAMPS

Family camp accommodations are often basic: cabins, university dorms, or rustic lodges are typical. But the programming can be really exceptional, whether it's the parent-child program at NASA's Space Camps in Florida, Alabama, or California, or Cornell University's summer program for families, which is held in Ithaca, New York, and offers courses from photography to history to wilderness skills. Some of these camps are all-together family affairs; at others, adults and kids split up during the day and reconvene in the evening.

BED-AND-BREAKFASTS

Once a destination for singles and couples only, more bed-and-breakfasts (B and B's) are beginning to accommodate families. Many of them—especially in the United States—still have a minimum age (few accept children younger than eight). Keep in mind that the majority of guests won't have children, and that they'll expect quiet evenings and mornings. The typical decor in a B and B is not very child-oriented—antiques and expensive furnishings are the rule rather than the exception. You should speak directly to the owners to get a feel for whether youngsters are really welcome.

There are many books, CD-ROMs, and Web sites listing specifics about these inns. A travel agent is little help with this type of accommodation, so be prepared to do some research on your own.

CAMPING

There's something about being in nature that brings out the best in adults and children. Maybe it's the peace of a nighttime sky or the camaraderie of sitting around a campfire. During the day, you can't help making wonderful discoveries, from the delicate intricacies of a spider web to the gnawed evidence of a beaver-felled tree. Camping is a low-cost getaway once you have the basic gear. It's also a vacation you can organize in a day, unless you're hoping

SIMPLY PUT...

ROOMS AND RATES

double/double, queen, king • Hotel rooms are categorized in part by bed size. A double/double room is equipped with two double beds, a queen has a queen-size bed, and a king has a king-size bed.

junior suite, suite • A junior suite usually offers a bedroom, a small living room, and a bathroom; a full suite is likely to have larger rooms and more than one bathroom.

rack rate • The rack rate is the published price for a hotel room—but it's a price you should rarely have to pay; there are almost always special rates and packages available.

to land a spot in the most popular camp-grounds on holiday weekends. Here's what you need as a bare minimum:

- A GOOD TENT WITH A RAIN FLY AND A GROUND CLOTH
- SLEEPING BAGS FOR EVERYONE
- COMFORTABLE PADS ON WHICH TO PUT YOUR SLEEPING BAGS
- A LANTERN AND FLASHLIGHTS
- COOKWARE, INCLUDING A SKILLET AND POTS IN SEVERAL SIZES, PLUS UTENSILS AND CLEANING SUPPLIES
- A DAY PACK AND WATER BOTTLE FOR EACH FAMILY MEMBER

There are campgrounds in national forests, in city and state or provincial parks, and throughout the national park systems. The amenities range from nothing to hot show-ers, flush toilets, restaurants, and stores. Privately owned campgrounds, such as Kampgrounds of America (KOA), often have more facilities; playgrounds, pools, and organized activities are common. A KOA or similar facility can be a terrific way to get used to camping if you are not comfortable in the wilderness, or if you

Rustic cabins *offer a way to feel close to nature without the discomforts of sleeping in a tent. They're also easier to lock up when you want to leave and go sightseeing.*

like sleeping in a tent but prefer a hot shower in the morning. Get a good direc-tory to find campgrounds or RV parks in North America; see page 142 for sources.

COTTAGES AND CABINS

Cottages and cabins are ideal for family vacations, and reasonably priced. Families can be active—boating, swimming, and hiking are typical activities—but you can also just sit on your porch, put your feet up, and watch the sunrise or the sunset. Cabins can be part of an enclave, or far away from it all. You can rent cottages all over the world or close to home, and stay for a weekend or for an entire summer. Before you rent, make certain you know what you're getting: Kitchen equipment, dishes, utensils, and bedding may or may not be included. Some waterside accom-modations include a boat, others don't.

CAMPGROUND HOUSEKEEPING

GETTING DOWN AND DIRTY WHILE YOU'RE CAMPING is definitely part of the fun, especially for kids. But it's nice to know that you can opt for being clean, comfortable, and organized when you want to. How? Bring the right accessories. Here's a range of camping gear that gives outdoor-loving families the best of both worlds.

You don't need clothespins *with this travel wash line; just pull the strands of the line apart to secure towels or clothes.*

Don't bother to hand-dry dishes; *put them in a net bag, hang it up, and go have fun. Leave dishes in the bag until the next meal.*

A hanging solar shower *is a welcome luxury at the end of a long, dirty day.*

Whether you're camping, *canoeing, or rafting, few items are as comfortable as these lightweight folding chairs.*

A whisk broom *and dustpan can keep tents and cars dirt-free and are small and light enough to tuck in anywhere.*

For information on rental sources, call the chamber of commerce or tourism department in the area you want to visit and ask to have a copy of the local paper—with classified ads—sent to you. Local newspapers may also list vacation rentals. Check with local and national parks, too.

THEME PARKS

A theme park can offer a remarkably stress-free vacation because it's hard to think about work or worries when you're screaming down a roller-coaster track. Some parks, most notably Walt Disney World in Florida, are world-class destinations on their own, with hotels, golf courses, and campgrounds. The main decision to make in a place like Walt Disney World will be whether your priority is to save money (by staying outside the park) or time and travel (by staying inside the park).

RELATIVES' HOUSES

What's great about staying with relatives is the bargain price and the chance for children to get to know their extended family. What's not great is how stressful it can be if you and your relatives aren't in sync. The way to minimize conflict is to talk about expectations in advance so you won't be disappointed and your relatives won't feel put-upon. Resolve such issues as who will babysit for your children when you're not there, how to handle discipline problems, whether kids can have between-meal sweets, and how late kids can stay up. Talk to your children about helping around the house and being respectful of relatives' routines. If it seems as though

things could be problematic, consider visiting for a couple of days and then staying at a nearby motel for a few more days.

VACATION HOMES

Many families opt for condos or houses because they provide a lot of space for the money. Rental homes allow several generations or more than one family to vacation together. Condos and homes may or may not have maid service; you may have to pay extra for it. Some villas, particularly those in the Caribbean, come with someone to cook and clean up or babysit, and some even have kids' programs. There isn't a downside to this kind of vacation unless you're expecting something you don't get. Ask the owner or the rental agent about services and amenities before booking.

Home exchanges work if you live in a place that people want to visit and if you have a home that meets the standards set by agencies.

There are companies dedicated to arranging apartment- and home-stays. Still others set up home exchanges—you give your home to a family while you take theirs. This low-cost arrangement works if you live in a place that people want to visit and if you have a home that meets the agencies' standards (well-furnished, clean, and in a safe place). If you're uneasy about opening your house to strangers, swap homes with friends who live in an interesting location. Check travel magazines and newspaper travel sections for ads and listings.

KID STUFF

---*---

M ANY RESORTS, HOTELS, CRUISE SHIPS, RANCHES, AND FAMILY CAMPS NOW OFFER SUPERVISED CHILDREN'S PROGRAMS, AND THE NUMBER AND SCOPE OF SUCH PROGRAMS HAS INCREASED DRAMATICALLY IN RECENT YEARS.

This means that parents and children today have more choices than ever about how to spend their vacation time.

LEARNING AND FUN

There are many reasons to use a good children's program while you're vacationing. First, it's an excellent way for your kids to meet other children from around the country or even around the world. These programs can also introduce your children to sports, such as tennis, that might not interest you but might well appeal to your children.

The benefit of these programs isn't confined to the kids either. While your

Good children's programs keep kids happy and teach them new skills.

children are safely and happily joining in games and activities set up for their age level, you can indulge in some of the things adults like but kids usually don't, such as playing golf, shopping for souvenirs and clothing, browsing in museums intended for adults, attending a seminar or a concert program, or reading by the pool without interruptions. When you have a chance to do these things with your partner or friends and you don't have to drag the kids along, everyone has a better day.

Finally, remember that a good supervised children's program will teach kids about a place or culture in fun, entertaining, educational, and age-appropriate ways. Counselors are usually local people who know and love the area they live in. They can provide an insider's view of a place; stories and legends about a natural or historical site; facts about flora, fauna, and wildlife; and sometimes an introduction to native dress, languages, or cuisine.

WHAT TO WATCH FOR

On the other hand, not all programs are created equal. Parents should drop in while programs are in session before their kids attend to make sure all is well. (For questions to ask about a children's program, see the checklist on page 134.) Some counselors and programs are excellent; others are not. There are many variables, but the quality of a program may be in question if many age groups are lumped together, if counselors spend more time talking to

Don't enroll your child in a program where safety is taken lightly, or where counselors are unwilling to discuss parents' concerns.

one another than to the children, if kids spend most of their time watching videos, or if scheduled activities are often canceled. Don't enroll your children in a program where safety seems to be taken lightly or ignored, or where counselors are unwilling to discuss parents' concerns.

Most vacation programs don't have officially mandated guidelines, which is why there's such a range in quality and

why parents have to check out programs carefully. One important consideration is the ratio of adults to children; this is regulated in most day-care centers, but it's generally not regulated in resorts. This ratio is a major safety issue, especially if counselors take children near the pool or beach. Before enrolling your children, check to see that the program meets these ratios provided by the National Association for the Education of Young Children:

◆ MAXIMUM OF 3 INFANTS TO 1 ADULT

◆ 6 OR FEWER TODDLERS PER ADULT; NO MORE THAN 12 TODDLERS IN A GROUP

◆ 10 OR FEWER PRESCHOOLERS PER ADULT; NO MORE THAN 20 IN A GROUP

◆ 15 OR FEWER SCHOOL-AGE CHILDREN PER ADULT; MAXIMUM 25 IN A GROUP

Keep in mind that while a good children's program is a terrific opportunity for kids, it is not a substitute for family time.

SIMPLE SOLUTIONS

SITTER SENSE

HAVING TIME TO YOURSELF ON A FAMILY VACATION does not make you a bad parent. It makes you more relaxed and helps you de-stress. Whether you plan ahead or take one day at a time, check into the availability of sitters and children's activity programs.

Simple

Decide each morning whether you'll want adults-only time, then arrange for sitters or use children's programs accordingly. Stay flexible in case space is unavailable or plans fall through.

Simpler

Determine ahead of time when you'll want to take off for adult pursuits. When you make your reservations at the hotel or resort, also reserve sitters or space in children's programs.

Simplest

Bring your own sitter. If you don't have one who can join you on vacation, take along the teenager of a relative or friend. Some ranches and family resorts have special "nanny" rates.

Eating Out, Eating In

---***---

Vacation time often revolves around food. The good news is that when you're on vacation, you have more time to enjoy meals and a chance to be adventurous in what and where you choose to eat.

Even cooking is different on vacation; it's more relaxing because you don't have the normal constraints of tight—and conflicting—family schedules. Vacation is a time to loosen up a little; your kids will not suffer if they don't have balanced meals every day and they won't wind up at the doctor's office if they eat more ice cream than fruit. The same goes for adults.

WHILE TRAVELING

It's fun to indulge in an occasional feast at a gourmet restaurant if it strikes your fancy. But simple, fast, and easy are good

Picnics are simple, yet they can be as stylish as restaurant meals.

words for family vacation meals. After all, in a spectacular setting the simplest foods seem anything but ordinary. Search for local restaurants and regional cuisine. A snack stand in a beach town serving fresh fish can be just as fast and inexpensive as a chain restaurant—and a lot more interesting. Local farm-produce stands are good places to pick up fruit and other snacks and to give kids firsthand knowledge about what grows in different areas.

Picnicking en route is a way to keep meals simple and give kids time to run around after sitting for long hours. If you don't want to pack food in advance, stop at local grocery stores along the way.

If you do decide on a fast-food joint, pick one with a playground or play space. You can eat and have a chance to talk with your partner while the kids exercise.

AT YOUR DESTINATION

Whether you're camping or staying at a five-star resort, find food solutions that make sense for your family.

If it's family time you're after, plan dishes the kids can help with; camping lends itself to this. Add fun to what you eat. Silly shapes and creative designs give even common food a little pizzazz and make kids more interested in helping. When your lodging includes a kitchen or an outside grill, you can get the family together in the late afternoon for conversation and cooking; one person doesn't have to do it alone.

Parents need adults-only time, and meals can be one way to get it. If you're staying at a resort or hotel, give the kids a treat by ordering their dinner from room service one night. If your children are old enough to stay in the room for a couple of hours by themselves, you can go down to an adults-only dinner, work out at the gym, get a massage, take a walk with your spouse, or sit in the hot tub. If they're too young to be left alone, hire a babysitter. If you have two separate rooms, let them eat and watch a movie in one while you relax in the other. If there is no room service, or if it's too pricey or doesn't offer food kids like, try ordering in a pizza from a local delivery place. Most hotels have no objection, and it can be a great cost-saver.

Sometimes what you need on vacation is a meal in minutes. You can cook simple fare such as hot dogs and hamburgers, or be a little silly and have breakfast for dinner one night: Cereal and fruit takes no time to prepare; pancakes or scrambled eggs and toast take just slightly longer.

Vacation is an opportunity to take the whole family out to one elegant meal if that's something you don't usually do at home. Parents are often surprised by how grown-up their children can be, all dressed up with someplace special to go. Pick a place that won't take all night to serve you, though. Even when they love what they're doing, children have a fairly limited capacity for sitting still.

THERE'S NO NEED TO OUTDO YOURSELF WHEN COOKING ON THE ROAD—EVEN THE SIMPLEST MEALS SOMEHOW SEEM TASTIER IN A NEW SETTING.

Dinner dumplings
When everyone has spent the day hiking or boating and is ready for a hearty meal, a one-pot dinner is in order. Heat your favorite canned stew to boiling, then drop baking-mix biscuit dough by spoonfuls on top. Cover and cook until the dough has a light, breadlike texture.

Breakfast bears
On a leisurely morning at the campsite, cooking can double as entertainment: Just whip up some batter from a pancake mix and let the kids help you drop it onto the griddle in fun shapes, such as these bears. Add nuts, raisins, blueberries, or chocolate chips for decoration if you wish.

Who Knew?

These days some hotel minibars are electronically controlled, so even if you just move—but don't consume—any of the drinks and snacks, you could end up getting charged for them. To avoid this, ask that the minibar be emptied before you arrive.

If sticking to a budget is your goal, buy inexpensive foods your kids like and cook them more than once while you're away. If you're staying in a hotel, rent a refrigerator and stock it with snack and breakfast foods so you don't have to eat in restaurants so often. Decide in advance how many meals you'll eat out and stick to that—even if the kids whine about it. Let them know that by saving on meals you'll have extra money to spend on one more fun activity for the whole family.

Not everyone wants to cook on vacation, and yet eating every meal with the whole family in a restaurant can be a budgeting nightmare. If you want to take a vacation from cooking but don't want to spend a fortune, choose an all-inclusive resort or adventure vacation that covers breakfasts, lunches, dinners, and snacks in the base price. Such vacations include ranches, cruises, rafting and canoe trips (among other adventure possibilities), and stays at many family camps and resorts.

If you just want to get a handle on food expenses, you can prepay for a meal plan at many places. Also, some packages include meal options. Research trips that let you take care of these costs up front.

Families traveling to foreign countries have an eating adventure in front of them. If your children like adventure, that's great. Try new foods together and find recipes for your favorites so you can re-create them back home. If your kids aren't adventurous, you can usually find something they'll like in the restaurants of international hotels, and—for better or worse—McDonald's is almost everywhere now.

Your kids may or may not handle rich and spicy foods well. If you're going to Mexico, for example, you might want to introduce them to the cuisine gradually by taking them to a Mexican restaurant before the trip. Don't ask your children to finish every meal; you could spend the rest of the evening taking care of a child with an upset stomach. Do be cautious about

If your children like adventure, try new foods together and find recipes for your favorites so you can re-create them back home.

foods in countries where the water may be unsafe: Eat only well-cooked foods and avoid any uncooked fruits or vegetables unless they haven't been peeled and you can wash them (with bottled water) and peel them yourself. Don't use the ice cubes, either, unless you're staying in an international resort with a purified water system (most of the resorts in Mexico's major tourist areas now fall into this category).

COMPACT COOKING

✳

WHEN YOU'RE CAR CAMPING, you can bring many of the com-
forts and conveniences of home with you. There's no need
to rough it with beat-up cookware and gear; today's campers can
stock their kitchen—whether it's on wheels or in the woods—with
gear that's as shiny and sleek as it is compact.

Fold-up stoves *are better for the environment
than campfires and take up little room in a car.*

A small chopping board *will protect RV and
camper counters, let you cut and chop with ease,
and make cleanup quick and simple.*

Insulated mugs *keep hot beverages
toasty even on a chilly morning.
Some mugs have snap-on covers to
prevent spills while you're driving.*

The best cookware *for camping is a nested set of pots
and pans with fold-up or removable handles; pots that
don't nest take up more space. Some sets come with a
lid designed to fit snugly on a variety of pot diameters,
so you don't have to carry more than one lid.*

FILLING your VACATION with STRESS-FREE Fun

—※—

1 Sign up for **family camp** with your children, and have meals and activities provided for you. **2** Pick a **sport** you've never tried, such as sailing or skiing, and learn it together. **3** Bring along a ball and play **catch** with your kids. **4** Work beside biologists, archeologists, or paleontologists, digging or observing **in the field.**

5 Join a **ranger program** or take part in a science workshop at a national park. **6** Visit living-history museums, where kids can **see and feel** the past as people lived it. **7** Take your cue from the road and stop at any **interesting site** you pass, whether it's a junkyard or a historic battlefield. **8** **Keep it simple:** Collect shells or leaves, pick berries, observe bugs, or watch birds.

9 On your way to **view autumn leaves,** stop and explore old cemeteries and **make rubbings** of interesting gravestones.

10 Preserve your vacation **memories** while still on vacation by creating journals, scrapbooks, photo albums, videos, and collages. ●

GETTING IN A FULL DAY'S PLAY

LIVING IT UP WITHOUT STRESSING OUT

In an ideal world, parents would have time to do everything that needs to be done, plus a lot of time left over to have fun with their children. Unfortunately, between work and shopping, driving and picking up, cooking and cleaning, and keeping the house in good repair, the one thing that we don't seem to have time for is the very thing that's most important to us and to our children: time to play together.

Vacation, however, is that ideal world, one in which you can play with your kids as long and as hard as you like. There are all kinds of ways to play on vacation, from goofing around to organized camps and classes, from walking hand-in-hand on a beach to challenging each other to reach a new level of technical skill in a sport you all love. The bottom line is that you can't go wrong with any fun activity. Whatever you do and however you do it, you and your children will be better off for having taken the time to play together.

ACTIVITIES FOR EVERYONE

---✳---

VACATION DESTINATIONS OFTEN INCLUDE OPPORTUNITIES FOR SPORTS-RELATED ACTIVITIES. SOME YOU MIGHT PURSUE AT HOME; OTHERS—SUCH AS SCUBA DIVING—ARE THINGS PEOPLE DO MAINLY WHILE TRAVELING.

Vacation is an excellent time to hone the skills required for your favorite sport or to try learning a completely new activity.

SPORTS CLINICS

Families who want to immerse themselves in one activity can sign up for a camp or clinic. Many of these are designed specifically so parents and children can take them together. Outward Bound USA, an organization dedicated to teaching outdoor skills and building confidence in people of all ages, has a few parent-child courses in such activities as backpacking,

sailing, canoeing, rock climbing, and dog-sledding. If you like fishing, retailers Orvis and L.L. Bean both offer parent-child fly-fishing clinics each summer. L.L. Bean holds its clinics in Maine; Vermont-based Orvis has several locations in the United States. Both the Annapolis Sailing School, headquartered in Annapolis, Maryland, and the Offshore Sailing School, based in Fort Myers, Florida, have courses for families with all skill levels, some in Florida and the Caribbean. At Camp Seafarer in North Carolina, families can learn sailing or motorboating together.

SIMPLE SOLUTIONS

GAME PLANS

WHETHER YOU WANT TO BE YOUR CHILD'S primary instructor or a cheering fan watching from the sidelines, you will find that sports can bring parents and children together. Here are some strategies for planning your involvement.

Simple

If you are very accomplished in a sport, you feel you're a good and patient teacher, and your child shows an interest, take him or her to the courts, course, slopes, or field for lessons.

Simpler

Sign your child up for a clinic or two so he or she can master the basics, then offer lots of practice time with you to supplement the essential skills learned from the pros.

Simplest

Utilize multiday camps and schools to give your child consistent, professional instruction; then at the end of class each day, have your child show you what he or she has learned.

Having a ball while on vacation can be as
simple as playing catch at the beach.

Ski resorts are an excellent resource for sports camps and clinics. Whistler Resort, north of Vancouver, Canada, has snowboard, mogul, and ski-race camps, all of which take place on a glacier in summer. The tennis school at Smugglers' Notch, Vermont, is for both parents and kids, and Wintergreen Resort in Virginia gives parents and children their own special session at the Golf Academy.

ALL-AROUND PLAY

If you want to try a variety of sports while you're on vacation, consider going to an all-inclusive resort at which activities don't cost extra. One of these resorts, Club Med, offers a unique option: instruction in circus arts, including the high trapeze. Both kids and adults can take these classes; by the end of a week's vacation many of them are performing amazing moves high above the safety net. Whistler Resort in Canada also offers trapeze instruction.

Traditional hotels have options, too. Sometimes sports equipment is available at no charge; other times it's pricey. To stay within your budget, check out the hotel brochures or call before you go.

Contrary to their image as a scene for eating and sitting, sitting and eating, cruises often provide active shore excursions for passengers to choose from. While these do cost extra, you can take as many or as few as you like. American Hawaii Cruises is one with a terrific array of sports-oriented options: biking, snorkeling, kayaking, and more. But sometimes cruising families do

One unusual offering is trapeze instruction. By the end of a week, kids and adults are performing high above the safety net.

better budget-wise to arrange their own sports-oriented excursions. For example, at Kahalu'u Beach less than five miles from the port of Kona on Hawaii's Big Island, there's first-rate snorkeling with gear you can rent locally at a considerable savings over the ship's excursions.

Some types of vacations fall between clinics and resorts. Ranches, for example, are mostly about riding, and most include instruction; however, the schedule and lessons are not as structured as at camps.

GET RAIN-OR-SHINE CLOTHES THAT
ARE PERFECT FOR SWIMMING, HIKING,
BIKING, AND JUST GOOFING AROUND.

Quick-dry clothes
New fabrics have made life much easier on
outdoor-loving kids; they can now play in
the rain and snow without upsetting parents
because their clothing dries in a flash.

Fleece pullovers and vests
Fleece vests and jackets keep kids warm, dry
fast, and can be stuffed into a day pack. Take
one with you even if it's hot and sunny when
you leave camp in the morning.

Hiking boots
Don't skimp on these. If your kids will be
walking the trails, get high-quality boots
with strong support and traction, and don't
forget to waterproof them.

Water wings
These popular "floaties" cannot save your
child's life, but they can help young children
feel safer in the water. Remember: Never
leave kids alone, even in shallow water.

Go-anywhere sandals
You don't want to worry about your kids'
getting shoes wet or dirty, and sometimes
an impromptu adventure means they don't
have hiking boots on. The new breed of
sandals is at home in the river, on trails,
at the pool, or on the plane.

If you're on a working ranch or cattle drive,
you spend all of your time riding, but the
focus will be the ranch work rather than
the learning. That's not to say you won't
improve your riding skills as you go.

You can take scuba-diving trips on
boats around the world if you're certified;
or you can take a certification course. Children as young as 12 can become certified,
so this is an opportunity for you and your
children to learn diving as a family. Call
in advance to check on the courses offered,
requirements, and what kind of certification you'll receive: often it's best to do any
preliminary work at home and save the
"in-water" part of the course for vacation.
Also check on the minimum age requirements for diving students at that location.
Some diving resorts offer children's camps
for those too young to dive.

At a ski resort, families can head out
to the slopes and ski together, take a couple of lessons, or opt for a multiday ski
clinic. Decide whether any members of
the group would benefit from lessons, or
whether you'd rather learn on your own.

Biking Basics

Lots of vacation places have
bicycle rentals, but many don't
have children's bikes, baby seats,
or helmets available. Try to call
ahead to make sure they have
what you need so you and your
kids won't be disappointed.

THE SIMPLEST THINGS

Not every activity has to be a big deal or cost a lot of money. Sometimes the simplest things give us real pleasure. Take along a couple of mitts and balls, a Frisbee disc, or a football and play catch with your kids before dinner at the campground or cottage. If you keep a pair of binoculars handy, you and your child can stop and enjoy your vacation spot's unique flora, fauna, or architecture.

If you're vacationing near a stream or lake, grab your kids and sit by the water each afternoon to fish and talk. Whether you catch anything is less important than having time together. Many places have a "catch-and-release" regulation, so make sure that you are allowed to keep the fish you reel in. In the United States, adults usually need a fishing license, while children under age 15 (or sometimes a little younger) generally don't.

If you're traveling by car or RV, take along bikes on a bike rack so you have the freedom to stop and explore any inviting byway. Hotels often have bike rentals as well. Virtually every ski area has summer biking, either on local roads or on trails. To reach mountain trails, you hook your bike onto the chair lift and ride up with it—a part of the adventure that most kids like as much as the biking.

Other choices abound. You can go to a golf driving range while you travel or at your vacation destination, hit a few balls on your hotel's tennis courts when they're not busy, participate in an aerobics class if your resort has one, or just go for a family walk. Life on vacation is great.

children's SKI GEAR

KEEP YOUNG SKIERS WARM AND SAFE BY BUNDLING THEM UP IN THE RIGHT KIND OF CLOTHING AND GEAR.

Ski suits

One-piece insulated suits keep kids warm; snow can't sneak in even if kids roll around in it. Teach them how to undo the suit for bathroom breaks, though.

Helmets

Your children wear bike helmets; they should wear ski helmets, too. Yes, skiing is a safe sport, but head injuries are possible and ski schools require helmets. If kids start wearing them when they're young, they won't think twice about it as they grow older. Have the salesperson fit the helmet properly.

Sunglasses or goggles

The glare of the sun on snow can be fierce, so eye protection is an absolute must. Many instructors won't admit kids to ski school without either glasses or goggles.

Mittens and gaiters

Mittens are warmer than gloves. Like other clothing, they should be high quality and waterproof. Leg gaiters aren't crucial, but they can help keep snow out of boots.

LEARNING ON LOCATION

———— ✳ ————

Travel is always a learning experience. Every time you talk with someone from a distant city or country, every time you look out over a landscape different from your own, you learn something.

But if you want to make the learning more concrete, there are dozens of ways to do so—whether you sign up for a multiday workshop or make a quick stop at a roadside monument. Don't underestimate your child's willingness to learn; the world is an exciting place and children want to understand how it works. Be forewarned, though: Children do not always learn in the ways we think they should; they have their own ways and their own time frame.

SUMMER WORKSHOPS

Universities are among the many institutions offering courses for families. The University of California, Santa Barbara; Pennsylvania State University; Cornell University; and Indiana University at Bloomington all have summer programs aimed at families. Universities outside the United States have similar programs. At some, children and adults learn together, at others they have separate activities by day and get back together in the evenings. Courses cover a huge range of topics, so if one school doesn't offer what you want, try another. Generally, you needn't be one of the school's alumni to sign up.

Families interested in science have a lot of choices. They can work side by side with paleontologists digging for dinosaur bones, or with archeologists excavating Native American sites. Earthwatch, a nonprofit organization in Massachusetts, puts

Vacations offer great opportunities
to expand your knowledge.

volunteers on research sites around the world to help scientists studying people, animals, history, sociology, and the environment. Some projects combine sports like snorkeling and diving with research; on others you can use your artistic talents to provide sketches of what you see each day. The minimum age for working with Earthwatch is 16, but other organizations accept younger children.

Many programs at or near national parks are oriented toward the sciences. The Yellowstone Institute in Yellowstone National Park has field courses and nature-study vacations. On the Galápagos Islands, a national park of Ecuador, rangers and naturalists show how and why Charles Darwin created the core of his theory of evolution when he was studying there.

Nature programs of all kinds abound. The Sierra Club and Appalachian Mountain Club both have dozens of outdoor programs, most for parents and children, some aimed at grandparents and grandchildren. These groups' outings focus on

No matter what you wish to learn, there's a place you can take your family for a weekend or a week to fulfill your dream.

low-impact, basic camping skills; nature studies; and the environment. One of North America's best-known organizations for this kind of program is the National Wildlife Federation (NWF). The NWF's annual Conservation Summits have long given families the time and place to learn

Educational programs *abound at museums around the world. Here, kids at the British Museum learn with the help of computers.*

and play together. Summits take place in various locations around the country during the summer months.

Arts, languages, and history are also well represented among family workshops. Adults and children learn to play instruments, sing, dance, write, paint, draw, and perform at places such as the International Music Camp Summer School of Fine Arts in North Dakota, Arkansas's Ozark Folk Center, West Virginia's Augusta Heritage Center, and the Chautauqua Institution Summer School in New York. Canada's Whistler Resort has a summer language camp, and the Hostelling International group offers family trips to a number of European countries, where adults and children not only explore but also learn about Europe's fascinating history.

No matter what you wish to learn, there's a place you can take your family for a weekend or a week to fulfill your dream. Several travel books, including some listed on page 142, provide more information about learning vacations that are designed specifically for families.

LIVING HISTORY

Throughout the United States are houses where U.S. presidents have lived, played, or worked, and libraries and museums devoted to their lives and accomplishments. Going through the exhibits and rooms doesn't require a major time commitment, but the power these places have to engage kids' minds is inspiring. At Abraham Lincoln's house in Springfield,

Living-history museums may be places of learning, but you'll never convince kids of that; these museums are just too much fun.

Illinois, you can touch the very banister Honest Abe touched each and every time he climbed up or descended his stairs. In Abilene, Kansas, you can see the pillows that Mrs. Eisenhower embroidered for each of her boys, including future president Dwight David, and the room that Ike shared with his brothers. The short

film at the Eisenhower Center gives children an understanding not only of the president but of what world leaders were thinking and doing during World War II.

Living-history museums are another window onto the past. Virginia's Colonial Williamsburg may be the most famous in the United States, but there are historical locations throughout the world, like Conner Prairie in Indiana and Old Sturbridge Village in Massachusetts. No trip to Stockholm, Sweden, would be complete without a visit to Skansen, an outdoor historical museum and zoo.

What's great about living-history museums is that they take history out of the pages of books and put it in front of you so you can really experience a sense of the past. They may be places of learning, but you'll never convince children of that fact; these museums are just too much fun.

Once upon a time, *kings built grand castles that remain as links to the past. You can tour many of them, including Mad King Ludwig's Neuschwanstein in Bavaria.*

Other countries have castles and dungeons, crown jewels, ancient ruins, and mythical gods and goddesses for inquisitive children to discover. You can explore battle sites, tombs, old ships, and places where ghosts have been known to walk. Learning places include zoos, aquariums, natural history and children's museums, and wild-animal parks. Boring? No way.

WORKADAY WONDERS

Sometimes learning happens in unexpected places. If an opportunity presents itself, by all means take advantage of it. Have you ever seen how the lock system on the mighty Mississippi works? Some locks have recorded information you can listen to as you watch massive barges rise and fall with the water level.

Dams on rivers in the Northwest have ladders built into them so fish can swim upstream to their spawning grounds; some fish ladders have underwater viewing areas to let you watch part of the journey. Places such as these don't cost a cent to visit, but they give kids—both big and little—a lot to learn and think about.

There are working mines and mills that welcome visitors. You'll never see wheels bigger than those on the massive trucks at the Kennecott Copper Mine outside Salt Lake City, Utah, and that sight alone is reason enough to visit.

You can go down into a coal mine in Beckley, West Virginia; it's no longer operational, but the tour guides are former miners, and they'll tell you stories about what it's like to work in a mine. On summer tours at the Pacific Lumber Company

Book It!

A reliable guidebook is the best travel companion for any family. It can tell you what's worth seeing (and what isn't) and give you tips on getting around. Carry a regional series if you're driving through more than one area; a single-destination guide if you're going to stay put.

in Scotia, California, you don't just hear stories, you actually see mill workers on the job. What most visitors remember, though, is the debarker's awesome power as it sprays water under enormous pressures to strip the bark from giant trees.

Along back roads and highways are ghost towns, small museums, factories, and plants with tours; there are interesting bridges and buildings, and places where famous people once walked. There are communities where natural or human disasters left a permanent mark for future generations to learn from.

Not every interesting site has an advertising budget or a public relations firm to bring attention to it. If you keep your eyes open and your schedule flexible enough to allow detours, you and your children will find intriguing places to visit in each and every corner of the world—many of them not too far from your home. Some of these adventures you may recall years from now, as you look back on your family's best vacation moments.

VACATIONS FOR ALL SEASONS

---✳---

EVERY SEASON HAS ITS TREASURES FOR TRAVELERS, AND IF THERE IS ONE THING CHILDREN ARE GOOD AT, IT'S FINDING RICHES OTHERS CAN'T SEE. SOME OF THE BEST—AND LEAST EXPENSIVE—FAMILY ACTIVITIES INVOLVE THESE.

Fun family vacations are possible in all seasons of the year. They can be planned around sports, nature, or just plain fun.

WINTER

When we find it difficult to slow down, Mother Nature sometimes does it for us, keeping us inside when it's deep-down-in-your-bones chilly outside. If we're lucky enough to be away on vacation when that happens, we often find ourselves inside a lodge or condo, curled up on a couch with our kids, watching a fire and cuddling together to keep warm. A cold and blustery day is the perfect opportunity for

Fun teaching tools, *like these decorated arches, help kids learn to ski. Instruct your children yourself or enroll them in classes.*

that downtime every vacation should have. But sometimes Mother Nature can make winter so inviting that you just have to go out and explore. Family snowshoeing is a low-cost winter activity, and one practically anyone can master. Ask if there are any guided nighttime walks where you're staying. Tromping across an expanse of moonlit snow will open your eyes to even more wonders in the wintry world.

Ranches and ski areas often will have horse-drawn sleigh rides in the daytime and nighttime. If you and your children have never experienced dashing through the snow in an open sleigh, you're in for a real treat. Drivers provide cozy blankets, and you generate another kind of warmth: singing, laughing, and wonderment at the lovely, old-fashioned ride.

If the rush of downhill skiing isn't for you, consider cross-country, or Nordic, skiing, a calmer, quieter, and less expensive way to slide on snow. Many downhill areas also have Nordic centers, with equipment, instructors, and groomed trails. Before heading out, pick a trail that's not too long or too difficult for the least experienced member of your group. Carrying an exhausted or freezing child is hard, if not impossible, on skis. Unlike downhill

Make a record of the natural wonders you discover while traveling.

skiing, cross-country doesn't require much specialized gear; bundle up in layers, with a moisture-wicking layer next to the skin.

Don't forget old-fashioned sledding. It's still as much fun as when you were a child—maybe even more so when you share the experience with your kids. And if you want to have a real adventure, ski areas and outfitters from Maine to Alaska offer dogsledding. Depending on the outfitter and the kind of adventure you sign on for, you may just want to sit and enjoy the ride, or learn to mush your own team.

SPRING

You can vacation right from home in the spring. Walk in the woods; visit a pond or wetlands region; climb a hill; visit a city park—you'll be surprised what you find there. In New York City's Central Park visitors have spotted parrots and peregrine falcons who have made their home there.

Resorts all over the world have nature activities for children and families; many naturalist-led walks and talks are free or moderately priced. Wintergreen Resort in

Virginia has a stellar environmental program that includes nature walks and other activities families with children of all ages can join. Always check to see if the hotel you're visiting offers similar programs.

For many families, spring break means walks by the seaside. Pack a mesh bag to collect shells. Let your children take their time and make their own discoveries. The main goal is to have fun; if they get a science lesson on the way, it's a side benefit.

Take Only Pictures

Collecting is fun, but it's not allowed everywhere. In national parks, for example, you cannot remove even a rock, stick, or fallen bird's nest; and picking flowers is definitely against the rules. Encourage your kids to take a picture, write a description, or make a drawing instead.

NATURE ACTIVITIES

✴

A WALK IN THE WILD—OR EVEN THE NOT-SO-WILD—can be a journey of discovery when children have the tools they need to explore and create. That doesn't mean you must buy a lot of fancy stuff. On the contrary, good, basic gear and equipment is best. After all, it's not the gear that counts, it's what kids do with it.

Kids can make *a field journal using a notebook with a pad of paper and pockets to hold pens, scissors, and a magnifying glass.*

Ready-made curio cabinets *(sold at hardware stores for organizing nuts and bolts) can house rocks, shells, and other treasures.*

An explorer's pack *holds a butterfly net, compass, magnifying glass, binoculars, nature guide, and other tools for observing the natural world.*

Kids can preserve *summer blooms using a flower press they make themselves from boards and blotting paper or newsprint.*

SUMMER

Fat, juicy berries say "summer" in the most delicious way. Berry picking is hands-on learning at its best, and you can eat the "information" as you go. If you know a place near home where wild berries grow —and where you're allowed to pick and you know the berries are safe—make that the destination of your next family day trip. While you're traveling, keep an eye open for "U-Pick" farms across the land.

Don't leave home without a bug house and magnifying glass; the world is alive with insects (there are more of them than us), and kids have a natural attraction to things that creep, crawl, and fly. There are many excellent nature books for children. Look through the selection at your local children's bookstore and pick those that are right for your kids. Get yourself a good adult field guide, too, so you can identify creatures that aren't included in the children's guides. Don't forget to bring a good pair of binoculars; let your kids explore with these. Do tell children always to put the strap around their neck (so that they don't drop and break the binoculars), and to let bugs go after studying them for a while.

Hiking is a low-cost family adventure, which is just one reason it is among the most popular outdoor vacation activities. If you're visiting national or state parks, get a trail map when you arrive and pick

Buy a bug cage *(or make one) so young naturalists can observe an insect up close—then set it free.*

the two or three best trails for your family. Read descriptions and distances aloud and let the kids help choose. You want them interested in where you're going and what you're seeing. Pack supplies to keep your family safe, warm, and well fed even if it's just a short hike, then take to the trails. You may be passing through a park for only a single day, but by walking the footpaths and seeing the land close up, your family gains a real sense of the place and begins to understand why someone felt this was an area worth preserving for generations to come.

Join ranger-led hikes, too. They're free and you always learn something. When parks have marked trails with numbered signs to learn as you go, pick up the appropriate pamphlet and stop at each marker; let the kids take turns reading the information out loud to the rest of the group. And if you're hiking without a ranger and see wild animals roaming in a park or a forest, don't try to get close to them no matter how tame and approachable they may appear. Teach your kids that the best way to care for nature and wildlife is to have as little impact on them as possible.

FALL

Fall is a terrific time to be outdoors with your family, and there are usually great opportunities for getaways over long holiday weekends. Less expensive and easier to

A weekend jaunt in the country
can be fun as well as fruitful.

plan than a full-scale vacation, weekend trips to the city or country can be just the ticket to revitalizing you and your kids for the winter holiday season.

While driving through the countryside on your way to pick apples or visit a pumpkin farm, why not stop and explore old cemeteries? Find historic gravestones and make rubbings of the inscriptions, but take care not to disturb or damage any of the artifacts. If you're in a location where someone famous is buried, investigate the person before or after you go; for a writer, take turns reading one of his or her works aloud while you're there.

Leaf "peeking" is an autumn tradition in places like New England, where various hardwoods change their foliage from cool green to brilliant reds and golds. You don't have to trek into the woods to appreciate them; many of the most beautiful trees stand alongside country roads and highways. Like shell collecting in summer, leaf collecting can be fun for the whole family, but do it only where it's allowed, and be discriminating: You don't want to take home the entire forest floor.

Although summer is when most families visit living-history museums and nature centers, autumn programs abound at such places, and the nearby lodging is often less expensive than in summer. Look for museums celebrating the fall harvest; they may demonstrate old-fashioned cider making, for example. Nature spots may offer fall walks where migrating birds stop to rest. In the United States, many living-history museums celebrate Thanksgiving; go and find out how the Pilgrims cooked and prepared for this fall event.

Capturing the Moment

W HEN YOU GO ON A VACATION YOU LOVE, YOU WANT TO FIND WAYS TO PRESERVE THE IMAGES AND IMPRESSIONS FOREVER. PHOTOGRAPHS ARE THE MAIN WAY MOST FAMILIES DO THIS, BUT THERE ARE OTHER WAYS, TOO.

Be creative and encourage your children to think of ideas. Here are some different visual and written memory-makers to try:

◆ PHOTO ALBUMS

◆ JOURNALS

◆ SCRAPBOOKS

◆ MAPS SHOWING YOUR TRIP ROUTE

◆ SKETCHBOOKS

◆ POSTCARD COLLECTIONS

◆ FOUND-OBJECT COLLECTIONS

All of these are projects that children can complete on their own. Sometimes you may have to encourage them; if children don't make entries in their journals every day, it's not the end of the world.

Creating a joint family project can be a way to avoid hassles; if someone doesn't feel like participating one day, you'll still have a record of the day from other members of the group. Have kids update their journals while you prepare dinner at the campsite or vacation home. Or bring journals to the hotel dining room so kids can stay busy while waiting for food.

Families who camp in places other than national parks can work with found

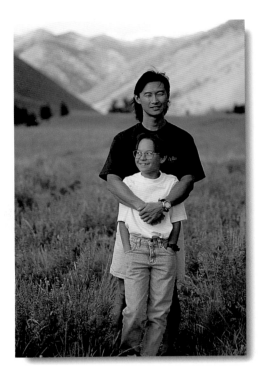

Together in a pleasant place: *What else could be a more fitting subject for photos to preserve in the family album?*

objects, including leaves and rocks. Glue leaves into a scrapbook (always carry a glue stick in your activity-supply kit) and cover the pages with plastic wrap. One nature-loving family hangs a piece of burlap at the campsite, then lets all family members fasten found objects onto it. The result—a living collage—is a wonderful record of their trip, burlap and all.

A family scrapbook may contain post-cards, found objects, brochures, trail maps, words you've seen on signs, photographs, sketches, or just about anything else that someone in your family wants to put into it. Leave it out and see what great memories and mementos are added.

Families visiting a big city can put together a joint photo album of architectural treasures such as gargoyles, manhole covers, decorative grates, and doorways—even tiled subway walls can have enough artistic appeal for a photograph.

If technology is what you love, bring a video camera in addition to one or more still cameras. You can supervise the use of expensive equipment, but let the children take turns being videographer and director; it gives you a chance to experience the vacation through their eyes. After you get back, plan an evening to watch the results. Make some popcorn, get comfortable on the sofa, and relive your good times.

Whatever you create or make from your journeys, don't stash it away in a drawer or closet to be forgotten. Hang it up on a wall or lay it out on a coffee table; put it on a bookshelf in a well-used family area. Every now and then, you and the kids can take it out, look, laugh, and reminisce. Even if you can't get away again for a while, your family can hang on to the sense of discovery you enjoyed and the connections you created on a memorable vacation.

Photo Ops

Give each child an inexpensive or disposable camera to photo-graph your trip. As film rolls fill up, have them developed at one-hour photo labs at places you stay. That way, your kids can make a vacation scrapbook as they go along—and create a souvenir that's hard to top.

CHECKLISTS
AND RESOURCES

INFORMATION FOR TRAVELING FAMILIES

* —— * —— *

When it comes to planning a family vacation—even a simple one—it's hard to be sure you've thought of everything. That's because anytime you travel, especially in the company of children, there's a lot to think about.

Toward that end, the pages that follow offer a selection of helpful checklists you can use whether you're driving or flying, vacationing at a resort, or embarking on a wilderness adventure. Listed in this section are the right questions to ask in a variety of situations, a sample itinerary, and a range of products—from first-aid supplies and kids' activity kits to clothes and sports equipment—to meet the needs of travelers of all ages. You'll also find books and organizations of interest to traveling families, as well as contact numbers for travel and tour programs mentioned in this book.

Refer to the lists just as they are, or use them as a starting point for creating your own personalized lists and itineraries.

Choosing a Travel Agent

———— ✳ ————

Travel agents who really know and understand the family market are rare. If you're satisfied with your travel agent's answers to these questions, you're in luck—you've found a good one.

- Do you have children of your own and do you travel with them?

- Do you frequently book family trips? Can you put me in touch with a client who can provide a reference?

- Are your recommendations based on firsthand knowledge and personal experience? Client feedback? Hearsay?

- Is your agency a member of the American Society of Travel Agents or another professional organization?

- Does the hotel, resort, or cruise line you're recommending have a supervised children's program? For what ages is it intended, and when does it run? (Also see checklist on page 134.)

- Are cribs and rollaway beds available? Is there an extra charge?

- Can you give specific reasons why this destination is good for *my* family?

- Why are these rates so low? Is it the rainy (or other less desirable) season?

- Are there any hidden or additional fees from your agency (say, if I change my tickets) or at the destination (such as extra charges for children or mandatory tips and other gratuities)?

- What about refunds? If rates drop, will you reissue the tickets at the lower price? If my child gets sick and we cancel, can I get my money back?

- Does the car rental company you're suggesting provide child safety seats? At what additional cost?

- Will you send advance boarding cards with confirmed seat assignments for every member of my family?

- Will you get back to me with choices for children's menus, and then order them for all of our flights?

- Can you send a prepacking list or family tip sheet now? Two weeks before departure is too late for me.

- What entry papers and other documents are necessary for my family?

PACKING CHECKLIST

DON'T FORGET TO REMEMBER

———— ✳ ————

THERE'S A LOT TO KEEP TRACK OF, ESPECIALLY IF YOU'RE PACKING FOR BOTH CHILDREN AND ADULTS. A GOOD LIST WILL SAVE TIME AND PREVENT LAST-MINUTE WORRIES OVER WHETHER YOU'VE FORGOTTEN SOMETHING.

ESSENTIALS
- ☐ Tickets, itinerary
- ☐ Traveler's checks, credit cards, cash
- ☐ Reservation or record locator numbers
- ☐ Prescription glasses and medications
- ☐ Passports, vaccination certificates
- ☐ List of emergency contacts

CLOTHING
- ☐ Pants, shorts, shirts
- ☐ Sweaters and jackets
- ☐ Underwear and socks
- ☐ Swimsuits, cover-ups, sunglasses, hats
- ☐ Winter hats, gloves, long underwear
- ☐ Rain gear
- ☐ Shoes, sandals, boots
- ☐ Dress clothes

Don't forget to pack the insect repellent!

SUNDRIES
- ☐ Bandages and antiseptic pads
- ☐ Acetaminophen or other painkillers
- ☐ Sunscreen, insect repellent
- ☐ Anti-itch and sunburn-relief lotions
- ☐ Decongestant, antihistamine
- ☐ Hair-care supplies, hair dryer
- ☐ Toothbrushes, toothpaste, dental floss
- ☐ Tweezers, nail clipper, nail file
- ☐ Bottled water
- ☐ Towels if you'll be camping
- ☐ Diaper-changing items
- ☐ Liquid detergent
- ☐ Tissues

FOR THE KIDS
- ☐ Personal tape players, tapes
- ☐ Children's activities (see page 132)
- ☐ Snacks, gum
- ☐ Favorite toy/blanket

ACCESSORIES
- ☐ Day packs or fanny packs
- ☐ Travel alarm clock
- ☐ Plug adapter
- ☐ Sports and camping gear
- ☐ Flashlight
- ☐ Childproofing products (see page 133)
- ☐ Camera, film

AGE-BY-AGE ACTIVITIES

KEEPING TRAVELING KIDS HAPPY

————— ✳ —————

H ERE'S A BASIC LIST OF AGE-APPROPRIATE GAMES, ACTIVITIES, AND TOYS TO KEEP KIDS OCCUPIED ON THE ROAD AND AT YOUR DESTINATION. BE SURE TO BRING STUFF SACKS OR SEAT-BACK POUCHES TO STORE EVERYTHING IN.

INFANTS AND TODDLERS
☐ Plastic keys and other chewables
☐ Soft animals
☐ Large blocks that fasten together
☐ Vinyl stickers
☐ Puppets
☐ Plastic bath books
☐ Foam puzzles
☐ Toys that attach to a car seat
☐ Suction-cup toys for windows
☐ Plastic play mirror
☐ Toy phone

PRESCHOOLERS
☐ Magic slate
☐ Magnetic board with shapes
☐ Sticker books and play sets
☐ Washable markers and pad of paper (or coloring book)
☐ Book-and-tape sets
☐ Large-size playing cards
☐ Inexpensive camera
☐ Pipe cleaners
☐ Nature discovery books

SCHOOL-AGE
☐ Travel activity books
☐ Road maps
☐ Journal or diary

☐ Children's atlas
☐ Finger puzzles
☐ Magnetic travel games, such as checkers
☐ Washable markers or colored pencils and pad of paper
☐ Children's magazines
☐ Easy craft kits
☐ Trivia games
☐ Book-and-tape sets

TEENS
☐ Personal tape or CD player (preferably one they don't have to share)
☐ Their own tapes or CDs
☐ Magazines
☐ Crossword puzzles
☐ Maze books
☐ Card games
☐ Good camera, film
☐ Portable watercolor set

EVERY AGE
☐ Personal tape players with headphones
☐ Music of all kinds, books on tape
☐ Books, books, books—from board books to young-adult novels
☐ Board games the whole family can play
☐ Playing cards
☐ Sketchbooks and pencils

CHILDPROOFING

MAKING YOUR HOME-AWAY-FROM-HOME SAFER FOR KIDS

---　✳　---

JUST AS IT'S ESSENTIAL TO CHILDPROOF AT HOME, IT'S ALSO IMPORTANT TO TAKE SAFETY PRECAUTIONS AT HOTELS, CONDOS, AND OTHER VACATION PLACES. HERE ARE SOME AREAS TO CHECK AND PROTECT.

LIVING AREAS

☐ Place corner guards on sharp-edged coffee tables and other furniture.

☐ Place breakable knickknacks in a cabinet, then put safety lock on the door.

☐ Install outlet covers.

☐ Tie up hanging blind cords with rubber bands, string, or pipe cleaners.

☐ On tables or shelves, move heavy items that a toddler can pull down.

☐ Secure windows and doors.

☐ Install safety gates across accessible stairs, doorways, and balconies.

☐ Keep minibar locked, or have its contents removed by the hotel staff.

☐ Look for ashtrays and matches; place them out of children's reach.

☐ Remove fireplace pokers and other sharp or pointed implements.

BEDROOMS

☐ Check for closet doors that could pinch fingers; install doorknob covers.

☐ Move cribs away from windows or hanging blind cords.

☐ Replace a crib that isn't up to current safety standards (slats no more than 2$^1/_2$ inches [6cm] apart, mattress snug against sides of crib).

☐ Install drawer locks on any dresser drawers that can be pulled open easily.

BATHROOM

☐ Replace breakable drinking glasses with plastic cups.

☐ Check for superhot water; insulate tub spouts with inflatable covers.

☐ Install toilet-lid locks.

☐ If there's no rubber mat for the tub, use your own removable, nonskid patches.

☐ Put down a towel or rug on tile floors, which can become slippery when wet.

☐ Check for a secure place to store medications, mouthwashes, and cosmetics out of children's reach.

KITCHEN

☐ Remove stove knobs that small children can reach.

☐ Push any coffeepot or toaster (and its cord) to the back of the counter.

☐ Install child-resistant cabinet and drawer locks, even if cabinets and drawers have latches.

☐ Move cleaning products to high cabinets that children can't reach.

☐ Remove knives and other sharp objects from drawers that are accessible.

CHILDREN'S PROGRAMS

QUESTIONS TO ASK BEFORE SIGNING UP

———— ✳ ————

HOW CAN YOU TELL A GOOD PROGRAM FROM A POOR ONE? ASK QUESTIONS BEFORE YOU GO AND OBSERVE THE PROGRAM BEFORE AND AFTER ENROLLING YOUR KIDS. DON'T SIGN UP UNLESS YOU'RE HAPPY WITH WHAT YOU LEARN.

◆ Does the person who developed or heads the program, or do any of the counselors, have a degree in child development or early childhood education?

◆ What is the counselor-to-child ratio? (The ideal ratio is no more than 3 infants, 6 toddlers, 10 preschoolers, or 15 school-age children per counselor.)

◆ Is the program divided into appropriate age groups, or are children of different ages lumped together?

◆ Are counselors trained in child CPR, first aid, and lifesaving techniques?

◆ How up-to-date and in what condition are toys and equipment? Do toys appear hazardous in any way? Are outdoor play areas safe?

◆ Does the program make specific use of the environment so children learn about the people, plants, and animals that are native to the area?

◆ What is the ratio of outdoor activities to indoor activities?

◆ How flexible is the program in terms of parents' schedules (hours and days it's open) and children's needs (if a child can't participate in a certain activity, is there an alternative)?

◆ Is there a place where the children's program meets every day, or is it run in whatever meeting room or other space happens to be free?

◆ What kind of information do counselors and parents exchange (is there a form on which to note allergies, fears, or special needs; do counselors leave information about their location if they move around the resort)?

◆ Are parents welcome to drop in and observe the program at any time?

ADVENTURE OUTFITTERS

WHAT TO KNOW BEFORE YOU GO

BEFORE YOU BOOK AN ADVENTURE VACATION, MAKE SURE THE OUTFITTER IS WELL PREPARED IN TERMS OF SAFETY AND IS EXPERIENCED WITH FAMILY OUTINGS—AND BE CERTAIN YOU KNOW EXACTLY WHAT TO EXPECT.

◆ Is this trip safe and age-appropriate for each of my children?

◆ Will there be other children on the same trip? If not, can you recommend an alternative date?

◆ Have the guides who will be on this trip worked with children before, and if so, what age were the children?

◆ Do you provide gear and clothing, or must we bring our own?

◆ What if I want to participate in an activity that my child is too young for?

◆ What will the group size be?

◆ What emergency training and equipment do the guides have, and where is the nearest medical facility?

◆ Will insects be a problem?

◆ Does the trip menu include foods children like? What do a typical breakfast, lunch, and dinner consist of?

◆ Are taxes and tips included in the cost?

◆ How far in advance do we need to book our adventure?

Learn all you can before
starting your adventure.

EMERGENCY CAR KIT

SUMMER OR WINTER, IT PAYS TO BE PREPARED

---- ✳ ----

AN UNEXPECTED BREAKDOWN OR A SUDDEN BLIZZARD CAN LEAVE YOU STRANDED FOR HOURS OR EVEN DAYS. THESE ITEMS, STORED IN YOUR CAR OR CAMPER, CAN KEEP YOUR FAMILY READY FOR ROADSIDE EMERGENCIES.

AUTOMOTIVE

☐ Jumper cables
☐ Spare wiper blades
☐ Window scraper
☐ Basic tools (screwdriver, pliers, adjustable wrench)
☐ Extra windshield-washer fluid
☐ Extra radiator coolant
☐ Extra motor oil
☐ Traction chains or a bag of salt or sand
☐ Spare tire, properly inflated and in good condition
☐ Tire-changing tools
☐ Your vehicle's operating manual

SURVIVAL

☐ Area maps
☐ Compass
☐ Drinking water
☐ Matches in watertight container
☐ Candles or lantern
☐ Flashlight with spare batteries
☐ Dried fruits or nuts
☐ Camping stove and pot
☐ Blankets or sleeping bags
☐ Extra warm clothing (jackets, mittens, overshoes, and hats)
☐ Tent or tarpaulin
☐ Ground cloth or tarpaulin

☐ Small shovel
☐ Multifunction pocket knife

HEALTH AND HYGIENE

☐ First-aid kit, including scissors, gauze, adhesive bandages, antiseptic cream
☐ First-aid handbook
☐ Emergency supply of any medications needed regularly
☐ Paper towels
☐ Toilet paper
☐ Moist towelettes (for washing hands without water)

COMMUNICATION

☐ Flares
☐ Notepad and pencil
☐ Red flag or cloth
☐ Transistor radio with spare battery
☐ Cell phone or CB radio
☐ Automobile club's 24-hour phone number for roadside assistance
☐ Car insurance company's 24-hour emergency phone number

MISCELLANEOUS

☐ Duct tape
☐ Rags
☐ Coil of sturdy rope

Auto Maintenance

A PREVACATION CHECKUP FOR YOUR CAR

※

BEFORE YOU HIT THE ROAD, TAKE TIME TO MAKE SURE THAT YOUR CAR IS IN TOP CONDITION. THE CAR CARE COUNCIL RECOMMENDS THAT YOU (OR A MECHANIC) CHECK THE FOLLOWING PARTS AND SYSTEMS ON YOUR CAR:

☐ *Cooling system.* Check that coolant is at the proper level and rust free, and that cap and hoses are in good condition, with tight connections.

☐ *Drive belts.* Check their adjustment and condition.

☐ *Battery.* Check fluid level.

☐ *Engine.* Check the condition and adjustment of ignition and carburetion components.

☐ *Air filter and PCV valve.* Check that they are clean and in good condition.

☐ *Lights.* Check that headlights, taillights, brake lights, and directional signals are in good working order.

☐ *Windshield wipers.* Check arm and blade condition and the level of the washer fluid.

☐ *Tires.* Check their pressure, tread, and general condition; rotate if necessary.

☐ *Brakes.* Check to see if the fluid level and adjustment are correct; have a wheel removed to check the condition of linings and cylinders.

☐ *Suspension and steering.* Check the steering linkage, shock absorbers, wheel alignment, and balance.

☐ *Lubrication.* Check the engine, transmission, and power steering oil; lubricate the chassis; change the oil and the oil filter if needed.

☐ *Exhaust system.* Check the muffler, exhaust, and tailpipes.

Make an automotive to-do list and check it off before you go.

SAMPLE ITINERARY

AN HOUR-BY-HOUR, DAY-BY-DAY VACATION SCHEDULE

---- ✳ ----

YOU CAN USE THIS EXAMPLE OF A THEME PARK VACATION AS A GUIDE TO PLANNING YOUR OWN VACATION. ADJUST THE ITINERARY TO YOUR LIKING, BUT DO TRY TO WORK IN A DAY OR SO SIMPLY TO UNWIND.

SATURDAY TO SATURDAY

(Sunday to relax)

Your itinerary will vary depending on whether you have multiday passes and for how many days, what else there is to do in the area, and so on.

DAY ONE

7:00 A.M. Leave home in time to reach the airport for a 9:30 a.m. flight.

12:30 P.M. Arrive at the destination airport; pick up a rental car or take a shuttle.

2:00 P.M. Check into the hotel; confirm reservations for a dinner show on day two.

3:00 P.M. Explore the hotel and hang out around the pool.

6:00 P.M. Family dinner at an inexpensive hotel restaurant.

DAY TWO

8:00 A.M. Get to the theme park early; rent a stroller if necessary; go right to the most popular ride.

10:00 A.M. Give your kids snacks.

11:45 A.M. Go to theme-park restaurants early for lunch to avoid crowds.

1:00 P.M. Choose two more rides to go on or attractions to visit.

2:30 P.M. Return to the hotel.

3:00 P.M. Swim or nap.

5:00 P.M. Have a quick dinner in the hotel food court or deli restaurant.

6:15 P.M. Return to the theme park; go on rides that usually have crowds.

DUSK Get seats for evening fireworks or other shows.

9:00 P.M. Return to the hotel.

DAY THREE

8:00 A.M. Get to the theme park early.

10:00 A.M. Snack and sit; choose your next ride.

11:45 A.M. Arrive at the theme-park restaurants early.

12:30 P.M. Pick two shady or indoor attractions to visit.

2:00 P.M. Snack and sit; choose final ride.

3:30 P.M. Return to hotel; rest and nap.

5:30 P.M. Leave for special dinner show or other evening event.

9:00 P.M. Return to the hotel.

DAY FOUR

Sleep in this morning.

10:00 A.M. Swim at the hotel pool.

NOON Eat lunch poolside.

2:00 P.M. Go shopping for fun souvenirs in the hotel or nearby.

5:00 P.M. Put the kids in hotel children's program or get a babysitter.

5:15 P.M. Adults use the health club, read, get a massage, or just relax.

7:00 P.M. Adult dinner out.

9:00 P.M. Pick up kids from the children's program.

DAY FIVE

8:00 A.M. Get to the theme park early and go immediately to a ride you haven't been able to get to.

10:00 A.M. Snack and sit.

NOON Have a relaxing lunch at a popular restaurant.

1:30 P.M. To escape the heat, go on indoor rides, rides you'll get wet on, or rides in the shade.

2:45 P.M. Go back to the hotel to swim and nap; snack at the pool.

5:30 P.M. Shuttle back to the theme park; grab dinner at a snack stand or cafeteria-style restaurant.

6:15 P.M. Go to the most popular rides and shows.

8:00 P.M. Return to the hotel. Cuddle on beds and watch a little TV together.

DAY SIX

9:00 A.M. Go to another attraction in the area if there is one: an aquarium, a second theme park, a zoo, a wild animal park, and so on.

10:30 A.M. Snack and sit.

11:45 P.M. Eat lunch at a quick restaurant, rock 'n' roll theme place, or other restaurant older kids like.

1:00 P.M. Look for rides or exhibits in the shade; attend shows or special events.

5:00 P.M. Return to the hotel.

6:00 P.M. Take the kids to kids' program or let the sitter take them to the pool.

7:00 P.M. Adult dinner out at a nice restaurant.

9:00 P.M. Pick up the kids.

DAY SEVEN

8:00 A.M. Go to the park if you have a four-day pass; if not, sleep in.

10:30 A.M. Snack by the pool.

12:30 P.M. Lunch at moderate restaurant or poolside.

2:00 P.M. Pick final rides to go on, or try an activity around the hotel.

3:00 P.M. Shop at various stores.

4:30 P.M. Return to the hotel; take naps to refresh yourselves for an evening out.

6:00 P.M. Get dressed up and go out for a fancy family dinner; if you're in the park, go to any evening fireworks display or other special event you haven't gotten to previously. Stay out late.

8:30 to 10:00 P.M. Return to the hotel.

DAY EIGHT

Sleep in. Visit souvenir shops or go to the pool for one last swim if your flight is late enough. Fly home.

DAY NINE

Relax around the house, unpack, start laundry, take film in for processing, thaw dinners you froze before leaving home, and have an easy meal.

DAILY PLANNER

A FILL-IN-THE-BLANKS ITINERARY

———— ✳ ————

ORGANIZING EACH DAY OF YOUR VACATION IS A SIMPLE MATTER OF DECID-ING WHAT TO DO AND FINDING A TIME TO DO IT. JUST PHOTOCOPY THIS FORM—MAKE ONE COPY FOR EACH VACATION DAY—AND FILL IN THE BLANKS.

Vacation day number_____

THINGS TO DO TODAY

_____
_____
_____
_____
_____
_____
_____
_____
_____
_____

SCHEDULE

Morning

6:00 A.M._____
_____

7:00 A.M._____
_____

8:00 A.M._____
_____

9:00 A.M._____
_____

10:00 A.M._____
_____

11:00 A.M._____
_____

Afternoon

NOON_____
_____

1:00 P.M._____
_____

2:00 P.M._____
_____

3:00 P.M._____
_____

4:00 P.M._____
_____

5:00 P.M._____
_____

Evening

6:00 P.M._____
_____

7:00 P.M._____
_____

8:00 P.M._____
_____

9:00 P.M._____
_____

10:00 P.M._____
_____

11:00 P.M._____
_____

MIDNIGHT_____
_____

PERSONAL INFORMATION FILE

IMPORTANT NAMES AND NUMBERS

———————— ✳ ————————

KEEP YOUR FAMILY'S PERSONAL INFORMATION HANDY IN CASE OF EMERGEN-CIES OR THE THEFT OR LOSS OF VALUABLES. LEAVE ANOTHER COPY WITH A FRIEND OR RELATIVE WHO CAN FAX IT TO YOU IF YOU LOSE THE ORIGINAL.

Passport and/or birth certificate numbers for your family _____

_____

_____

_____

_____

Frequent-flyer numbers for your family

_____

_____

_____

_____

_____

Travel agent's name and phone number _____

_____

Health insurance policy number _____

_____

Health plan emergency number _____

_____

Pharmacy name and phone number _____

_____

Prescription numbers for any regularly taken medications _____

_____

_____

_____

Pediatrician's name and phone number

_____

Internist's name and phone number

_____

Auto insurance policy number _____

_____

Auto insurance emergency number _____

_____

Family attorney's name and phone number

_____

Serial numbers of traveler's checks _____

_____

_____

_____

_____

_____

Credit card numbers _____

_____

_____

_____

_____

Credit card loss or theft reporting number

_____

Hotel reservation confirmation number

_____

Airline record locator number _____

_____

RESOURCES

Looking for additional details and guidance? These publications, retail sources, and organizations can help make your family vacation more enjoyable. Also listed are phone numbers for travel programs mentioned in the text.

PUBLICATIONS

Arthur Frommer's New World of Travel
By Arthur Frommer and Pauline Frommer
(Frommer, 1995)

The Best Bargain Family Vacations in the U.S.A.
By Valerie Wolf Deutsch and Laura Sutherland
(St. Martin's Press, 1997)

The Best Family Ski Vacations in North America
By Laura Sutherland
(St. Martin's Press, 1997)

Great Family Vacations series
By Candyce H. Stapen
(Globe Pequot Press)

Fodor's Ballpark Vacations: Great Family Trips to Minor League and Classic Major League Baseball Parks Across America
By Bruce Adams and Margaret Engel
(Random House, 1997)

Great Nature Vacations With Your Kids
By Dorothy Jordon
(World Leisure, 1996)

Kids' London
By Francesca Collin
(Ward Lock, 1997)

Parents' Guide to Hiking & Camping: A Trailside Guide
By Alice Cary
(W.W. Norton, 1997)

Trailer Life Campground/RV Park & Service Directory: United States, Canada & Mexico
(Trailer Life, updated annually)

SUPPLIERS

L.L. Bean
(800) 221-4221
www.llbean.com
Clothing, outdoor gear, sporting equipment, and luggage.

Eagle Creek
(800) 874-9925
www.eaglecreek.com
Packing, travel security items, toiletry kits, and more.

Tough Traveler
(800) 468-6844
Backpacks, duffel bags, day packs, sleeping bags, backpack-style child carriers, parent packs, and more.

Gizmo Luggage by Tutto
(800) 949-1288
Kids' luggage in bright colors, two- and four-wheeled versions. Also available are accessory bags, day packs, and more.

Patagonia and Patagonia Kids
(800) 638-6464
www.patagonia.com
Outdoor gear for all ages.

REI
(800) 426-4840
www.rei.com
Outdoor clothing and gear for all ages, including packs, hiking boots, camping cookware, and more.

Practical Parenting
(800) 255-3379
www.practicalparenting.com
Travel-related items, including the I.D. Me disposable bracelet.

Toys to Grow On
(800) 542-8338
A catalog with lots of great toys, some specifically for travel.

Storytime Creations Cards Kit
(800) 557-8679
Award-winning activity kit with stickers, wipe-off cards, crayons, markers, and an idea booklet.

Berlitz Kids
(800) 243-0495
Book-and-tape series from noted language specialist, for ages 4–9. Also look for The Berlitz Kids Picture Dictionary. Check bookstores or call for more information.

Rand McNally
(800) 333-0136, ext. 2111
www.randmcnallystore.com
TripTracker journal and game book for ages 8 and up. Activity atlases and sticker books for younger kids. TripMaker vacation-planning software for the family to use together.

ORGANIZATIONS

HotelDocs
(800) 468-3537
www.hoteldocs.com
HotelDocs has doctors in 150 U.S. cities; can usually get a doctor to your hotel within 35 minutes.

International Association for Medical Assistance to Travellers (IAMAT)
United States: 417 Center Street
Lewiston, NY 14092
(716) 754-4883
Canada: 40 Regal Road
Guelph, Ontario, N1K 1B5
(519) 836-0102
Join and receive a worldwide directory of physicians, and fixed prices on medical services.

Travel Medicine Center
131 N. Robertson Boulevard
Beverly Hills, CA 90291
(888) 888-3816
Medical information, first-aid kits, health products for world travelers.

TOURS/PROGRAMS

American Hawaii Cruises
(800) 474-9934

Annapolis Sailing School
(800) 638-9192

Appalachian Mountain Club
(603) 466-2727

Augusta Heritage Center
(304) 637-1209

Camp Seafarer
(919) 249-1212

Chautauqua Institution Summer School
(716) 357-6348 (June–August),
(716) 357-6255 (other months)

Cornell's Adult University Summer Program
(607) 255-6260

Club Med
(800) 258-2633

Colonial Williamsburg
(800) 447-8679

Connor Prairie
(800) 966-1836, (317) 776-6000

Earthwatch
(800) 776-0188, (617) 926-8200

Eisenhower Center
(913) 263-4751

Hostelling International
(202) 783-6161

IU Bloomington Mini-University
(800) 824-3044, (812) 855-5844

International Music Camp Summer School of the Arts
(701) 263-4211 (summer),
(701) 838-8472 (winter)

Lincoln Home National Historic Site
(217) 492-4150

L.L. Bean
(800) 341-4341

NASA Space Camps
(800) 637-7223, (205) 837-3400

National Wildlife Federation
(703) 790-4363

Offshore Sailing School
(800) 221-4326, (941) 454-1700

Old Sturbridge Village
(508) 347-3362

Orvis Fly Fishing School
(800) 235-9763

Outward Bound USA
(800) 243-8520, (914) 424-4000

Ozark Folk Center
(501) 269-3851

Pennsylvania State Alumni College
(814) 865-5466

Rascals in Paradise
(800) 872-7225, (415) 978-9800

Sierra Club
(415) 977-5522

Smugglers' Notch
(800) 451-8752, (802) 644-8851

Tyler Place
(802) 868-3301

University of California at Santa Barbara, Family Vacation Center
(805) 893-3123

Whistler Resort
(800) 944-7853, (604) 664-5625

Wintergreen Resort
(800) 325-2200, (804) 325-2200

Yellowstone Institute
(307) 344-2294

INDEX

ACKNOWLEDGMENTS

ADDITIONAL PHOTOGRAPHY: **Woodfin Camp** 42 Dick Durrance. **FPG** 120 Josef Beck; 122 Frederick McKinney. **International Stock** 17 Peter Langone; 31 Lindy Powers. **Stock Market** 40 R. B. Sanchez; 80 David Stoecklein. **Tony Stone Images** 20 Lori Adamski Peek; 25 Val Corbett; 32 Bob Krist; 50 Suzanne & Nick Geary; 66 Mark Kelley; 72 Jack Dykinga; 88 Joe McBride; 119 David Joel. **Superstock** 79 S. Barrow. **Uniphoto** 128 Kate Ryan. **Westlight** 22 Warren Morgan; 36 Dallas & John Heaton; 74 Charles Philip; 76 Jeff Vanuga; 81 Walter Hodges; 103 Ron Watts. Author photo by Judith Phillips. SPECIAL THANKS: The publishers wish to thank the following people for their valuable help during the creation of this book: Desne Border, Nancy Carlson, Rick Clogher, Mandy Erickson, Ruth Jacobson, Dawn Margolis, Cynthia Rubin, Carrie Spector, Patrick Tucker, and Laurie Wertz for editorial assistance; Jan Collier for artist representation; Gigi Haycock for help with photo styling; Paul Rauschelbach for computing support; Sharon Smith for jacket design; Bill and Kristin Wurz for design assistance; Ty Koontz for indexing. Thanks also to the following sources for the loan of photographic props: Susan Philippbaar and Gandhia Beyeler at KinderSport (San Francisco, CA); Susan Lee at Mascot Metropolitan, Inc. (South San Francisco, CA), distributor of Tutto and Gizmo luggage; and Ed Hoffacker at Palo Alto Sport Shop & Toy World (Palo Alto, CA). AUTHOR'S ACKNOWLEDGMENTS: My thanks to my children—Kira, Molly, and Hutch—who have taught me all I know about being a traveling parent, and to Janet Goldenberg, for her thoughtful and inspired editing.